COVE SCHOOL PHONICS WORKBOOK

Vowel Digraphs

Letter Patterns & Word Analysis — Part 2

cab·in   ge   oi

ca·ble   kn   ir

ti·ny   au   ci

Joyce Dadouche, M.A.
Laura L. Rogan, Ph.D.
Janis Wennberg, M.A.

Cove Foundation, Winnetka, Illinois

SRA/McGraw-Hill
Columbus, Ohio

ISBN 0-02-686977-2

1 2 3 4 5 6 7 8 9 10 MAL 99 98 97 96 95 94

Contents

Review of Long Vowels Workbook

Read each word. Find the picture that matches the word. Write the word neatly below the picture.

yolk	bolt	hoe	pie	eight	pipe
book	bone	child	chill	one	bowl
cub	cube	scale	river	eighty	globe

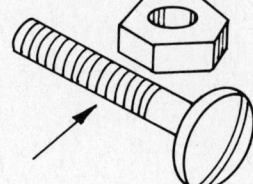

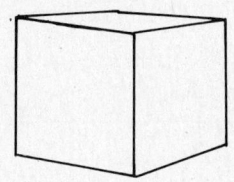

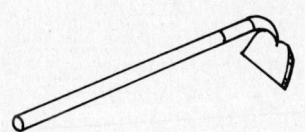

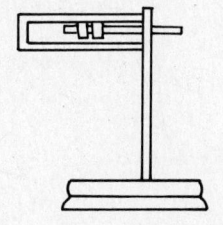

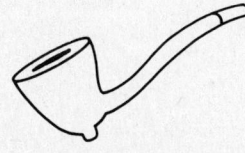

Review of Long Vowels Workbook

Divide (div·ide) each word into two parts. Circle the word that matches the picture.

whis·per whim·per whis·kers wis·dom		canteen cartoon carton costume		arrive army arrest argue	
ignore invent ignite igloo		contest comment compare compass		orbit organ order outlet	
bottom bottle butler button	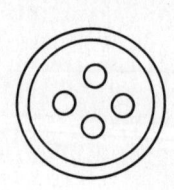	walrus welcome waitress welfare		perfect perform person perfume	
lumber number member slumber	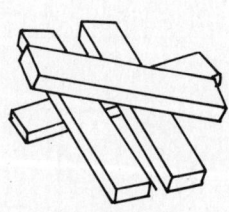	enter escape entire empire		winter willow whimper window	
trombone trinket trumpet tractor		campus canyon canvas cactus	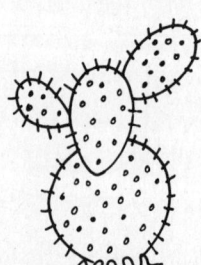	infant insect invite injure	

Review of Long Vowels Workbook — Contractions

Read the first two words and the contraction (con·trac·shun) they make when the words are put together. One or two letters are left out. Box in the letter or letters that are left out. Write them on the lines after the contractions.

you [wi]ll ⟶ you'll **w i**　　　　did not ⟶ didn't ___

we will ⟶ we'll ___ ___　　　　I have ⟶ I've ___ ___

they will ⟶ they'll ___ ___　　　that is ⟶ that's ___

are not ⟶ aren't ___　　　they have ⟶ they've ___ ___

can not ⟶ can't ___　　　there is ⟶ there's ___

Write the correct contraction for each sentence in the blank.

1. Next month _____ see if we get any green beans to eat from our garden.
we'll　we've

2. We told Dad that we _____ going to borrow his tools after all.
can't　aren't

3. We hope _____ like all these different kinds of candy.
you'll　you've

4. I feel sad to think that broken vase _____ be glued together again.
didn't　can't

5. Mom says little Arnold _____ go near that hot oven.
wasn't　mustn't

6. _____ see whose job it is to clean up this messy booth before we eat.
They've　They'll

7. Mr. Jones said _____ got to underline our spelling words in each sentence.
we've　we'll

8. When do you think _____ going to stop being so scared of the dark?
there's　he's

9. Carlos and Walter said _____ never seen that show before.
they've　that's

Write the two words that make up each contraction.

he's ___ ___　　hasn't ___ ___　　it'll ___ ___

hadn't ___ ___　　she'll ___ ___　　I'll ___ ___

wasn't ___ ___　　they've ___ ___　　he'll ___ ___

she's ___ ___　　there's ___ ___　　I've ___ ___

Review of Long Vowels Workbook — Contractions

Cross out the letter or letters that are left out when you put two words together to make a contraction. Then write the contraction on the lines.

has not ⟶ __ __ __ __ ' __   I will ⟶ __ ' __ __

have not ⟶ __ __ __ __ __ ' __   you have ⟶ __ __ __ ' __ __

is not ⟶ __ __ __ ' __   I have ⟶ __ ' __ __

must not ⟶ __ __ __ __ __ ' __   we have ⟶ __ __ __ ' __

they will ⟶ __ __ __ __ __ ' __ __   he will ⟶ __ __ ' __ __

she is ⟶ __ __ __ ' __   she will ⟶ __ __ __ ' __ __

Write the correct contraction for the two words under the first blank. Choose the correct word for the other blank and write it on the line.

1. We _____ find the plastic bucket we use to wash our _____.
   can not   bakes   bikes

2. _____ going to see a film about safety in school on _____.
   He is   Tuesday   trumpet

3. This is the coldest day _____ ever played _____.
   I have   ouch   outside

4. _____ one page in my spelling book that I have to _____.
   There is   finish   fish

5. _____ got to try to fly your kite on a _____ day.
   You have   windy   winding

6. _____ packing all her summer clothes because she's going on a _____.
   She is   trip   tip

7. _____ need to ask a question before she _____ her picture.
   She will   finishes   fishes

8. _____ put a circle around all the words that you need to _____.
   I have   story   study

Write the contraction for each set of words.

have not _____   she will _____   I will _____

is not _____   that is _____   are not _____

it is _____   you have _____   they have _____

they will _____   I have _____   there is _____

5

Review of Long Vowels Workbook

Read each sentence. Choose the best word for the sentence. Write it on the line.

You can hang your robe on a _____ in the closet.

Someone who gives a party is called a _____.

A car has this. You can lift up the _____ of a car.

host
hood
hoot
hook

When you have something in your hands, you _____ it.

When you dig with a shovel, you make a _____.

A tool for digging in the garden is a _____.

hoe
how
hold
hole

My little brother likes to be pushed in his _____.

Our kitten loves it when we _____ her neck.

Kate stubbed her bare toe on a _____ in the grass.

stone
stood
stroke
stroller

The bottoms of your boots have a heel and a _____.

The clerk at the hardware store _____ me some nails.

Dad used _____ lumber when he fixed the picnic bench.

sold
sole
soon
some

In the middle of an apple there is a _____.

Just before the sun rises a rooster will _____.

You may shiver if you are out in the _____.

cold
core
crowd
crow

A zig-zag line is a _____ line.

Someone who makes and bakes food is a _____.

Mom will give me a soft quilt to _____ my bed.

cook
cool
crooked
cover

Walter can't remember where he put his book of _____ tales.

Mom said, "I've got to _____ my clothes and put them away."

Dr. Polk told me that now I am fifty- _____ inches tall.

four
flow
folk
fold

© 1995 SRA/McGraw-Hill

Review of Long Vowels Workbook

Read the words in each box. Circle the word that matches the picture.

die doe do day	tool loud lock look	toe tea tie tow
coat code colt cold	blunt blink blind blend	swan snow snout snore
tea tie two toe	glee glow gold glue	plots post poke past
with wilt wind wild	owl out oat old	yolk joke folk gold
far form flour four	white while write wife	roll road rode raft

7

Review of Long Vowels Workbook

Read each sentence. Choose the best word for the sentence. Write it on the line.

He stood under the sprinkler to rinse off his _____ feet. The Saint Bernard dog whimpers _____ when his owner leaves. We'll go for a ride together after Dad _____ the horses.	sandals saddles sandy sadly
We _____ the little plants with care when we planted them. Mrs. Martin keeps a pen and note pad in a _____ spot. My father, brother, and I are left-_____, but my mother is not.	handy hamper handed handled
He wants to try to blow big, big _____. Yesterday we took my little brother for a _____ ride. The infant often sits in his crib and _____ to himself.	buggy bubbly babbles bubbles
There was just a _____ flower left on the rose bush. Mother didn't get mad. She _____ said, "You are late." Raking leaves isn't a _____ job if you do it well.	simply simple sample single
The scouts _____ the campfire and began to roast hot dogs. Ask your sister _____ if you may borrow her watercolors. That baker sold pies, cakes, and rolls, but not _____.	candle candy kindled kindly
The football players were _____ at the fifty yard line. She sprained her ankle and _____ to the bench to sit down. Mr. James likes to carve wooden ducks. It's his _____.	hobby hobbled huddled happy
Mrs. Post asked me to write eight words _____ on the board. Mom wants to mend my jacket, but she can't find a good _____. They ran in circles and got so dizzy they _____ fell down.	nearly needle needy neatly

1995 SRA/McGraw-Hill

Review of Long Vowels Workbook

1. These are the VOWELS.   **a e i o u** and sometimes **y**

2. The rest of the letters are CONSONANTS.   **b c d f g h j k l m n p q r s t v w x z** and sometimes **y**

3. Write all of the vowels. ____ ____ ____ ____ and sometimes ____

4. Write eight consonants. ____ ____ ____ ____ ____ ____ ____ ____

Write each of the words below in the correct list.

| folk | love | ape | have | picture | egg | where | yes |
| inch | one | toll | above | under | into | gold | use |

Words that Begin with a Vowel

_____ _____

_____ _____

_____ _____

_____ _____

Words that Begin with a Consonant

_____ _____

_____ _____

_____ _____

_____ _____

Fill in <u>vowels</u> to make real words.

t____p   b____ck   b____ne

c____t   l____ke   h____lp

t____ne   sh____p   b____ ____t

ch____p   th____nk   s____ng

Fill in <u>consonants</u> to make real words.

____ome   ____ie   ____old

to____   ma____   ____oot

____ane   ____ee   mou____e

boo____   mi____e   ba____ ____

Box in <u>the vowels</u> in each word.
Print the vowels on the lines.

s k y _____   a p p l e _____

w r i t e _____   r a b b i t _____

e i g h t _____   s a l e _____

t o p _____   o u t _____

m y _____   v e t _____

f o u r _____   u n d e r _____

Box in <u>the consonants</u> in each word.
Print the consonants on the lines.

y e l l o w _____   o f f _____

g a r d e n _____   y a r d _____

w i n t e r _____   z o o _____

f e l l o w _____   c o t _____

b u t t e r _____   p i g _____

n u m b e r _____   o u r _____

Review of Long Vowels Workbook — Compound Words

Read the words. Find the correct picture for each word. Write the word on the line.

beehive   footprints   notebook   tadpole   pineapple   wastebasket

_____	_____	_____
_____	_____	_____

Use the words below to fill in the blanks in the sentences. Read the words.

inside   outside   whenever   whoever   homemade   ourselves
anyone   whatever   understood   otherwise   everywhere   sometimes

1. Yesterday Grandmother served us freshly baked _____ apple pie.

2. Mom and Dad often allow us to play _____ until dark.

3. I'll share my ruler with _____ who needs it.

4. Mom said she'll cook _____ you want for dinner.

5. I do not think that small child _____ what you said to him.

6. We agreed to come _____ the house as soon as it begins to rain.

7. Joe and Andy looked _____ for the lost snow shovel.

8. Remember that _____ enters the contest will get a ribbon.

9. Vicky shivers _____ she gets very cold.

10. Mrs. Monroe told us that everyone makes mistakes _____.

11. They'll have to run quickly; _____ they'll be late for the show.

12. Steve and I can glue these two broken picture frames by _____.

Review of Long Vowels Workbook

Read each sentence. Circle the word that will finish the sentence.

The good seats are all taken, so the man said that I have to sit (here, hen, her).

When we go on a trip and we fly up in the sky, we are in a (plan, plate, plane).

For his own safety, that blind man uses a white (can, car, cane).

All our chickens are different colors, and they live in our (bare, bar, barn).

We will tie all those sticks of wood together with a (rode, rod, rope).

I haven't spoken to Mrs. Jones for eight days. I hope she's not (made, mad, make).

We are all going to the park, and I am going down the tallest (slip, slid, slide).

I finished shoveling the snow off the front walk and I am (glade, glad, glob).

Yesterday I swept the dining room rug after we (ate, at, all).

I didn't finish the last question, but the time was up, so I (quite, quit, quick).

Sometimes in class Steve and I write sentences that are the (same, Sam, son).

I wonder who is going to find the lost (kite, kit, kick).

I'll hold the tube while you glue the broken handle on the (cube, cub, cup).

It's cold this morning, so I'll have to put on my (robe, rob, rope).

I haven't taken the bus for so long I forgot how much the (fare, far, fan) is.

What is the matter with the car in front of us? There's so much (smoke, smock, smack).

Walter asked me to have lunch at his house, so I left Mom a (note, not, hot).

Shampoo comes in a bottle, and toothpaste comes in a (tub, tube, tug).

My brother is named Peter, but we all call him (Pete, pep, pet).

I'll go look at that horse with the pretty white (moan, mine, mane).

We are going to use this cloth to finish wiping the (tile, till, tilt).

Jenny will chop this Swiss cheese into small (cubs, cutes, cubes) for us.

Review of Long Vowels Workbook
Endings on base words that end with <u>e</u>

You remember this rule: When you add **-ed, -er,** or **-en** to words that end with <u>e</u>, you leave out one <u>e</u>, like this: smile + ed → smiled, bake + er → baker, froze + en → frozen.

Use the RULE above to add endings to the words below. Write the words you make on the lines. Read all the words.

Add **-ed**	Add **-er**	Add **-en**
rake _____	drive _____	take _____
pile _____	rule _____	gold _____
spell _____	skate _____	ripe _____
vote _____	stick _____	chose _____

When you read words like the ones below and you do not know the base word, how can you tell whether to say the vowel <u>name</u> or the vowel <u>sound</u>? You can look for this <u>letter pattern</u>: ONE VOWEL-ONE CONSONANT-ONE VOWEL. This pattern tells you to use the vowel <u>name</u>, like this: St|eve|n scr|ape|d his leg on the big r|ope|s.

Box in the VOWEL-CONSONANT-VOWEL pattern if you see it in the words below.

rider   used   robbed   taped   scraped   widen

spoken   tamed   robes   tapped   diver   bitten

Choose the words that belong in the sentences. Box in the <u>vowel-consonant-vowel</u> pattern before you write the words in the blanks.

1. The rabbits _____ to find fresh green leaves when they _____ into the garden. (h o p p i n g, h o p p e d, h o p e d)

2. The _____ _____ his truck out of the driveway. (b l o c k, b a c k e d, b a k e r)

3. Sue _____ the cream for the cake, and then she _____ the counter clean. (w h i p p e d, w h i n e d, w i p e d)

4. Luke needed a _____, some clips, and some _____ bands. (r u n n e r, r u b b e r, r u l e r)

5. Becky put the _____ food into the _____. (f r e e z i n g, f r o z e n, f r e e z e r)

6. They were _____ teams, and I was _____ to play with the Wildcats. (c h o s e n, c h o p p e d, c h o o s i n g)

Review of Long Vowels Workbook
Endings on base words that end with e

When you add **-ing** to a word that ends with e, leave out the e on the base word. This way you keep the one-vowel, one-consonant, one-vowel pattern.

To add **-ing** to these words: 1. Cross out the e.   2. Add **-ing.**
Write the word on the line.

trade _____   hope _____   hike _____

use _____   stare _____   poke _____

drive _____   brake _____   rule _____

Circle the correct word and write it on the line.

They do not like (driveing, driving) when there is so much traffic.   _____

Mom is (voting, voteing) for the person who'll do the best job.   _____

None of us will be (useing, using) these reading books today.   _____

The man will be (taking, takeing) pictures of our class next Tuesday.   _____

1. Choose the correct word for each sentence.   2. Take off the e.   3. Add **-ing**.
Write the word on the line in the sentence.

1. Don is _____ all his dimes and nickels in his bank.
   (save, shave, safe)

2. That man is _____ the rose bushes in his front yard.
   (pure, prune, plume)

3. Most of the logs in the campfire are still _____.
   (smoke, stove, spoke)

4. Our vet is very good at _____ sick dogs and cats.
   (cute, cube, cure)

5. Dad is _____ the front gate so our dog can't get out.
   (chose, close, choke)

6. They do not mind _____ that jar of silver paint.
   (square, shape, share)

7. Jan was outside _____ on the frozen puddles when she fell.
   (slide, slime, shine)

8. Digging coal or gold from underground is called _____.
   (mile, mine, mint)

Review of Long Vowels Workbook
Endings on base words that end with <u>e</u>

To get the <u>base word</u>, you take off **-ing** and put the <u>e</u> back on. Write the base words and their endings on the lines.

naming is <u>name</u> + <u>ing</u>   piling is _____ + _____

choking is _____ + _____   tuning is _____ + _____

scaring is _____ + _____   shaking is _____ + _____

diving is _____ + _____   stroking is _____ + _____

Box in the <u>vowel-consonant-vowel</u> pattern if there is one in the words below.

gliding	taming	dozing	bossing
waking	winning	shading	wiring
shedding	hosing	ruling	rusting
staring	hiding	starring	grading

In the questions below, circle the word that <u>ends</u> in **-ing**.
Write the <u>base word</u> that it came from on the line.
Read the <u>question</u> and circle <u>yes</u> or <u>no</u>.

1. Can you use skates or a sled to go biking? <u>bike</u> Yes No
2. Will Martin be joking if he feels sad? _____ Yes No
3. If it is afternoon, will the sun be rising? _____ Yes No
4. Do you ever see a little mouse chasing a big cat? _____ Yes No
5. Can Carmen go skating on a frozen pond? _____ Yes No
6. If I am blaming you, do you feel bad? _____ Yes No
7. If you jump on one foot, are you hoping? _____ Yes No
8. Are you caring for a pet if you give it water and food? _____ Yes No
9. Is Pete using a spoon to eat his sandwich? _____ Yes No
10. If Kate is very mad and upset, will she be smiling? _____ Yes No
11. Do you need an oven for baking? _____ Yes No
12. Can you jump off a diving board into a pool? _____ Yes No
13. If there's a thunderstorm, will the sun be shining? _____ Yes No
14. Is she asleep if she's taking a nap? _____ Yes No

Review of Long Vowels Workbook
Endings on base words that end with _e_

Read the words below and sort them into the correct lists. Follow the directions (der·ec·shuns) below.

1. Look for the vowel-consonant-vowel pattern. Box it in.   2. Say the **vowel name**.
3. Read the word. Write the word on the line if it belongs in the Vowel Name list.

lifting	bending	
roping	noting	
biting	quacking	
hunting	wilting	
wading	curling	
trusting	waving	
using	whining	

Vowel Name Word List

_____ _____
_____ _____
_____ _____
_____ _____

1. Look for the words that do not have the vowel-consonant-vowel pattern. Circle them.
2. Say the **vowel sound**.   3. Read the word. Write the word on the line if it belongs in the Vowel Sound list.

braking	melting
snatching	trusting
trimming	firing
timing	chopping
naming	poking
wedding	dusting
sunning	tuning

Vowel Sound Word List

_____ _____
_____ _____
_____ _____
_____ _____

Read the words in List 1. Circle the word in List 2 that has the same vowel sound as the underlined vowel in List 1. The sample shows you what to do.

List 1	List 2		List 1	List 2	
poking	(go)	got	slapping	A	at
packing	A	at	sloping	go	got
tilting	I	it	chiming	I	it
tiling	I	it	chinning	I	it
grazing	A	at	stocking	go	got

Review of Long Vowels Workbook — Endings on base words

Circle the word that belongs in the sentence.

We'll use that corkboard for (taking, tacking) up notes.

Sue said she'll give us all a cupcake to taste when she's done (baking, backing).

Cathy said a very fine singer is (staring, starring) in that show downtown.

The children were being silly and began (hopping, hoping) around like rabbits.

Look at that cute little kitten (starring, staring) at my goldfish.

He's all done (staking, stacking) his school books on the shelf.

I was told that they do not permit (smoking, smocking) anywhere on this train.

Here are some file folders to use for (filling, filing) those letters.

Mike went around in his wild ape costume (scarring, scaring) the other kids.

This Tuesday at four o'clock Mom is (taking, tacking) me to Dr. Holt for a checkup.

These long sticks will be good for (staking, stacking) those tall plants.

Come quickly! Dad is (baking, backing) the car out of the driveway for us now.

Joey said he wants to borrow my rake when I am done (racking, raking) these leaves.

The dentist told James that he has one tooth that needs a (filling, filing).

The two-year-old child began (fusing, fussing) as soon as his mother left.

Who is (planning, planing) on coming along with us to the picnic?

The hardest job was (scrapping, scraping) the old paint off the window sills.

Some glue spilled on her desk, and Mandy is (whipping, wiping) it off.

Mrs. Polk isn't going to begin (moping, mopping) the kitchen until we leave.

The children are (hopping, hoping) Miss Crane will read the folk tale they all like.

On Tuesday, Miss Rosen will give me my prize for (winning, whining) the art contest.

Take these books to Mr. Post when I finish (tapping, taping) the torn pages.

Review of Long Vowels Workbook — Endings on base words

Read each sentence. Choose the best word for the sentence. Write it on the line.

The children are _____ markers to draw pictures for the posters.	used
When Dad went to school, he _____ to study very hard.	user
Where is the wooden spoon Mom _____ when she mixes cake batter?	uses
	using
Mr. Larsen told everyone to smile when the pictures were _____.	take
She's _____ some freshly baked pies along on the picnic.	takes
Here is the cooler Steven _____ along on his camping trips.	taking
	taken
Mrs. Simms said that costume may _____ the small children.	scares
The small child was too _____ to ride on the roller coaster.	scared
Those two big barking dogs were _____ little Tommy.	scare
	scaring
We must go to the corner to cross the street _____.	safe
Whenever we go in the car, we have to put on _____ belts.	safer
Dad says this life jacket will be _____ than that inner tube.	safety
	safely
When he was little, Richy _____ showing his hermit crabs to us.	loves
Rose said the blue velvet dress in the store window looked _____.	lovely
Roller-skating is one of the sports my brother _____ the most.	loving
	loved
When you play baseball, there are many _____ you must follow.	ruled
Mrs. Morton said you may borrow her _____ in art class.	ruler
The umpire _____ that the last pitch was a strike.	rules
	ruling
The children stood by the goldfish bowl and _____ at the fish.	stare
Mr. Kroll asked Jake to stop _____ out of the classroom window.	staring
Mom and Dad told us that it's rude to _____ at others.	stares
	stared

Syllables

Longer words look hard to read, but they can be easy if you divide them into parts called syllables (sil·lu·buls).

A SYLLABLE is a word or part of a word that has one vowel sound.

Circle the correct word and fill in the blanks to complete the sentences below.

Pin has (one, two) vowel. The vowel letter is ____ .
The vowel sound that you say is like the vowel sound in (I, it).
Pin is a one-syllable word because it has one (vowel, consonant) sound.

Pine has _____ vowels. The vowels are ____ , ____ .
Do you say two vowel sounds in pine? (yes, no)
The one vowel sound you say in pine is like the vowel sound in (I, it).
Pine is a one (syllable, sentence) word because it has one vowel (sound, letter).

Say the words below softly to yourself. Think about how many vowel sounds you say in each word. Then answer (an·ser) the questions.

	How many vowel letters do you see?	How many vowel sounds do you say?	How many syllables are there?
can	_____	_____	_____
cane	_____	_____	_____
goat	_____	_____	_____
robe	_____	_____	_____
sneeze	_____	_____	_____
cut	_____	_____	_____
cute	_____	_____	_____
moose	_____	_____	_____
paint	_____	_____	_____
please	_____	_____	_____
shut	_____	_____	_____
shout	_____	_____	_____

Some of the words above have _____ vowel. Some of the words have _____ or
_____ vowels. All of the words above are _____-syllable words.

The number of syllables must be the same as the number of vowel (letters, sounds).

Syllables — Compound Words

Some longer words are made from two one-syllable words put together, like
flag + **pole** → **flagpole**. These words are called <u>compound words</u>.

> To divide a COMPOUND WORD, you divide between the two small words that
> make up the compound word. Those two words are called <u>syllables</u>.

Follow the directions below. Then circle the best word for the sentence.

Use a line to divide the words below into 2 one-syllable words.	Write the syllables on the lines below.	Write the number of vowel letters in syllable 1, syllable 2.	Circle the word with the same VOWEL SOUND that you say in syllable 1, syllable 2. Read the syllables.

rai|l|road   _____ • _____   _____ • _____   A, at • go, got

A <u>railroad</u> is used for   tracks   trucks   trains   tractors.

---

haystack   _____ • _____   _____ • _____   A, at • A, at

A <u>haystack</u> is a neat pile of hay on a   horse   tractor   farm   porch.

---

seaweed   _____ • _____   _____ • _____   me, met • me, met

<u>Seaweed</u> is a   fish   plant   water   seasick.

---

grapevine   _____ • _____   _____ • _____   A, at • I, it

A <u>grapevine</u> has   drink   purple   grabs   leaves.

---

firefly   _____ • _____   _____ • _____   I, it • I, it

A <u>firefly</u> is a kind of   bonfire   flower   insect   infant.

---

snowdrift   _____ • _____   _____ • _____   go, got • I, it

A <u>snowdrift</u> is snow piled up by the   sun   wind   melt   winter.

Circle the one-syllable words.

breathe   teabag   scratch   eight

porch   notebook   stroke   outside   spine

Syllables — Two middle consonants

Syllables in most longer words are not words themselves, but you can say the syllables because they have a vowel. <u>Mag</u> is part of <u>magnet</u>. **Mag** is not a word, but it is a syllable because it has a vowel. <u>Spl</u> is part of <u>splinter</u>. **Spl** is not a word or a syllable because it has no vowel.

Answer the questions below. Circle the words that make the sentence true.

1. Is there a vowel in <u>char</u>? _____ Is <u>char</u> a syllable? _____

   <u>Char</u> (is, is not) a syllable because it (has a, has no) vowel.

2. Is there a vowel in <u>scr</u>? _____ Is <u>scr</u> a syllable? _____

   <u>Scr</u> (is, is not) a syllable because it (has a, has no) vowel.

3. Is there a vowel in <u>trig</u>? _____ Is <u>trig</u> a syllable? _____

   <u>Trig</u> (is, is not) a syllable because it (has a, has no) vowel.

4. Is there a vowel in <u>nts</u>? _____ Is <u>nts</u> a syllable? _____

   <u>Nts</u> (is, is not) a syllable because it (has a, has no) vowel.

> Use this RULE to divide the words below into syllables. When a word has <u>two consonants in the middle</u>, you divide between those two consonants.

Follow the directions below. Then circle the best word for the sentence.

Use a line to divide the words into syllables.	Write the syllables on the lines.	Write the vowel that you see in syllable 1, syllable 2.	Circle the word with the same VOWEL SOUND that you say in syllable 1, syllable 2. Read the syllables.
trum|pet	_____ • _____	_____ • _____	blue, up • me, met
A <u>trum|pet</u> is something that you	read play eat throw.		
cactus	_____ • _____	_____ • _____	A, at • blue, up
A <u>cactus</u> is a	person tool insect plant.		
album	_____ • _____	_____ • _____	A, at • blue, up
An <u>album</u> is used for	picnics pictures pretzels pages.		

Circle all the syllables.   trm   gar   mup   shrp   nev   whrl   bliz

Syllables — Two middle consonants

You remember that a syllable may have more than one vowel letter, but the letters must stand for just one vowel sound.

Divide the words below into syllables. When two vowels like ea, ee, and oo are together, and you read them with one vowel sound, write the two vowels together.

Follow the directions below. Then circle the best word for the sentence.

Use a line to divide the words into syllables.	Write the syllables on the lines.	Write the vowel or vowels that you see in syllable 1, syllable 2.	Circle the word with the same VOWEL SOUND that you say in syllable 1, syllable 2. Now read the syllables.

canteen _____ • _____   _____ • _____   A, at • me, met

You use a <u>canteen</u> for something to   camp   eat   drink   connect.

---

treatment _____ • _____   _____ • _____   me, met • me, met

You may get a <u>treatment</u> when you go to a   party   game   store   doctor.

---

igloo _____ • _____   _____ • _____   I, it • blue, up

An <u>igloo</u> is a small   glue   insect   house   snow.

In syllables like -vite and -cade, the vowels are not together, but because they work (werk) together, they belong in the same syllable.

Write the vowels in the words below like this: trombone → _o_ • _o-e_ . The dash (-) tells you a letter has been left out. Do the rest of the page the same way as above.

---

mistake _____ • _____   _____ • _____   I, it • A, at

Try not to make a <u>mistake</u> when you   sleep   stumble   write   mister.

---

stampede _____ • _____   _____ • _____   A, at • me, met

<u>Stampede</u> may mean a herd of running   cars   feet   stamping   cattle.

---

costume _____ • _____   _____ • _____   go, got • blue, up

You may need a <u>costume</u> if you act in a   story   play   funny   cotton.

Syllables — Words ending with -le

When you divide words that end in a consonant and -le, like little, use this rule.

> RULE: Keep the consonant that is just before -le with the le, like this:
>
> apple **ap|ple**   candle **can|dle**   eagle **ea|gle**

Say these syllables slowly to yourself and listen to the way they sound.

	-ple	-dle	-gle
Do you say a sound for the letter l?	yes	no	
Do you say a sound for the letter e?	yes	no	

You do not say the vowel e in these words because l and e together are a team that gives you the vowel sound that you need for a syllable.

Box in the consonant -le pattern in these words. Write the syllables on the lines.

s a m p l e _____•_____   n o o d l e _____•_____   j u n g l e _____•_____

b e e t l e _____•_____   d r i z z l e _____•_____   p o o d l e _____•_____

t w i n k l e _____•_____   b e a g l e _____•_____   r a f f l e _____•_____

t u m b l e _____•_____   a n k l e _____•_____   t r e m b l e _____•_____

The letters ar, er, and or are vowel-consonant pairs that work together as a team. Keep them together in a syllable.

Use a line to divide the words below. Write the syllables on the lines.

t a r g e t _____•_____   c a r p o r t _____•_____   t h u n d e r _____•_____

p e r f e c t _____•_____   m a r b l e _____•_____   p a r t y _____•_____

d o c t o r _____•_____   c o r n e r _____•_____   b o r d e r _____•_____

g a r g l e _____•_____   c o r r e c t _____•_____   p e r f e c t _____•_____

Use these words to fill in the blanks: vowel   syllables   words   one   say

1. You can divide words into _____.

2. When you put syllables together, you have _____.

3. All syllables must have a _____ that you _____.

4. A word may have _____ or more syllables.

Syllables — Summary of Rules

Rules for Dividing Words into Syllables

I. A word with <u>one vowel sound</u> is a <u>one-syllable word</u>. A one-syllable word is <u>never</u> divided.

praise   fly   bite

2. Divide a <u>compound word</u> between the two words that make up the compound word.

milk|shake   mail|box   pop|corn

3. When a word has <u>two consonants in the middle</u>, divide between the two consonants.

rab|bit   hel|met   trac|tor

4. When a word ends in a <u>consonant</u> and -le, divide just before that consonant.

puz|zle   can|dle   noo|dle

Read the words below slowly so that you can hear the vowel sounds. Divide the two-syllable words. Write the number of the RULE you use for all the words.

	Rule		Rule		Rule		Rule
march	1	goggles	___	penny	___	crumble	___
prob|lem	3	toothpaste	___	true	___	these	___
bathrobe	___	scoreboard	___	thermos	___	startle	___

Read the syllables below. Then find the other syllable you need to finish these words. Write the second syllable on the line.

per_____   puz_____   wal_____   ea_____

side_____   spar_____   plen_____   lum_____

-kle   -son   -walk   -rus   -zle   -gle   -ber   -ty

Read each sentence. Use one of the syllables below to complete the word that follows the sentence. Write the syllable in the blank.

-tist   -zan   -ble   -flakes

I. This is something good to eat with milk. ....corn_____

2. This is someone who takes care of our teeth. ....den_____

3. This is something that you can do with eggs. ....scram_____

Words with three middle consonants

Some words have <u>three consonants in the middle.</u> Most of the time you can divide these words between the first and second consonants. Looking for consonant pairs helps, too.

Look for three consonants in the middle of the words below. Divide the words between the first (ferst) and second consonants. Then box in these consonant pairs: **st, gr, dr, sp.** Follow this sample: 1. in|stant 2. in⸢st⸥ant

hungry   hundred   congress   angry   monster   inspect

pilgrim   hamster   lobster   instant   address   children

Divide the words below into two syllables. Divide them between the first and second consonants. Keep the consonant pairs together. Write the syllables on the lines.

lobster is _____ • ___ ___ ___ ___

children is _____ • ___ ___ ___ ___

inspect is _____ • _____

angry is _____ • _____

hundred is _____ • _____

hamster is _____ • _____

pilgrim is _____ • _____

address is _____ • _____

monster is _____ • _____

hungry is _____ • _____

Words with three middle consonants

Here are some more words to divide after the **first** middle consonant. After you divide the words, box in these consonant pairs: **th, tr, fl, pl.** Read the words.

contract   filthy   inflate   explore   farther   subtract

Divide the words below into syllables. Then write the syllables on the lines. Keep the consonant pairs together. Read all the words.

attract   inflate   ostrich   panther   nostril   explode

attract is _____ • _____

ostrich is _____ • _____

panther is _____ • _____

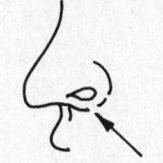

nostril is _____ • _____

explode is _____ • _____

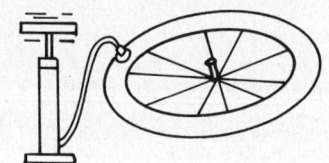

inflate is _____ • _____

In some words like the ones below, you divide after the **second** middle consonant. Divide the words. Then box in these consonant pairs: **th, mp, nt, rt, sk.**

pumpkin   muskrat   antlers   partner   athlete   empty

Write the syllables under the correct pictures as you did above. Read the words.

athlete is _____ • _____

antlers is _____ • _____

muskrat is _____ • _____

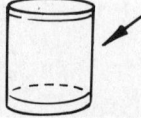

empty is _____ • _____

Words with three middle consonants

Divide the words below into syllables. Write the words neatly under the pictures.

nostrils	hundred	address	complete	mattress	antlers
monster	complain	hungry	partners	actress	explore
inflate	pilgrim	attach	panther	subtract	ostrich

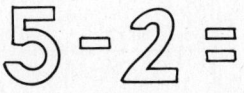

_____

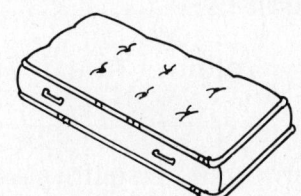

_____

_____

_____

_____

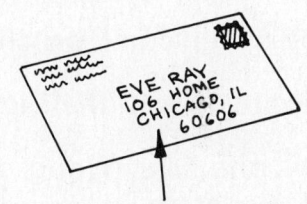

_____

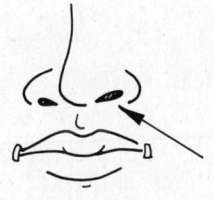

_____

_____

_____

_____

_____

_____

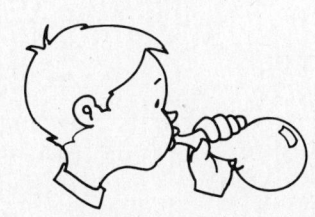

_____

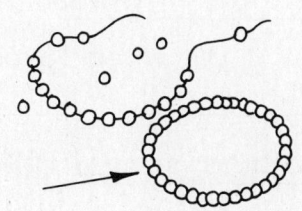

_____

_____

Words with three middle consonants

Find the syllables that will complete these words. Write them on the lines.

mat_____	com_____	mon_____
north_____	part_____	muf_____
un_____	sub_____	king_____
ant_____	pan_____	in_____
-ern, -cle, -tress, -lers	-tract, -plain, -ther, -ner	-ster, -clude, -dom, -fler

Fill in the correct word for each sentence. Use the words above.

1. Some deer have very big _____.

2. We sleep on the _____ in our bed.

3. My sister can't watch _____ pictures on TV because they scare her.

4. I want to see the big black _____ at the zoo.

5. Mr. and Mrs. Wang are going to take a trip to the _____ part of our state.

6. We each choose a _____ when we go on a class trip.

7. We have to get another _____ for our car.

8. Carmen had to add and _____ on the math test she took yesterday.

9. The king was fair in ruling his _____.

10. My _____ Dave is coming to our house for dinner.

11. Mom and Dad do not like it when we _____ about our chores.

12. He'll invite all his classmates. He will _____ everyone.

In the sentence below, circle the word that means to end or to finish something.

My mother likes to conclude our Thanksgiving dinner with pumpkin pie.

Circle the word that means to tell about in words.

It was hard for me to describe how it felt when I won the contest.

Circle the word that means that nothing is missing.

Our English teacher is showing us how to write complete sentences.

Words with three middle consonants

Find the syllables that will complete these words. Write them on the lines.

ex _____   mer_____   in_____

ex _____   ham _____   hun_____

far_____   ad_____   in_____

nos _____   pil_____   Eng_____

-ther,   -plore,   -dress,   -grims,   -gry,   -stinct,
-trils,   -press   -chant,   -ster   -lish,   -stall

Fill in the correct word for each sentence. Use the words above.

1. While we were camping, we took time to _____ the woods around us.

2. When you send someone a letter, you need to put an _____ on it.

3. The fastest way home is to take the _____ lane of the freeway.

4. The holes in your nose that you use for breathing are called _____.

5. The _____ sailed in a ship called the Mayflower.

6. If you haven't eaten in a long time, you are _____.

7. The drugstore is _____ from our house than the bank.

8. A person who owns or runs a store is often called a _____.

9. Someone who comes from England is _____.

10. The wheel that the _____ runs on squeaks as it spins around.

11. Beavers have an _____ to make dams with trees they have cut down.

12. It will take all morning to _____ the muffler in our car.

In the sentence below, circle the word that means to keep someone out.

He twisted his ankle, so the coach had to exclude him from the football game.

Circle the word that means to fill with air or gas.

Luke wants to borrow a pump to inflate the tires on his bike.

Circle the word that means to make something bigger.

Our teacher needs to increase the number of desks in our room because we have more children.

28

Words with three middle consonants

Write the correct word in each blank. If you cannot read a word, divide it into syllables.

lobby   lobster   loudly   locker

It lives in the sea and has a shell. _____

hamper   hamster   dryer   hungry

This is where we put clothes that need to be washed. _____

instant   increase   inspect   install

The firemen came to _____ our school to see that it is safe.

monthly   monster   Tuesday   Monday

The day after Sunday is _____.

hungry   hundred   ninety   nineteen

This is the number after ninety-nine. _____

pilgrim   panther   pumpkin   pattern

This is orange and we carve it to make a jack-o'-lantern. _____

Andy   angry   empty   any

When someone is very mad, he is _____.

attract   address   antlers   actress

Peggy acts in plays and on TV; she is an _____.

panther   pantry   oven   paddle

This is part of a kitchen where we keep food. _____

father   farther   fatter   faster

On weekends I sometimes go bowling with my _____.

anklet   antlers   athlete   actor

Someone who is very good at sports is an _____.

simple   simmer   summer   someone

If something is not hard to do, it is _____.

Sight Words I: people, animal, their, family, woman, women

Read the sentences. Try to read the word in the box. The meaning of the sentence will help you. In the rows below each set of sentences, circle all the words that are the same as the sample word.

Here is one person.   ⟶   Here are many | people |.

| people | people | purple | people | poodle | people | peephole | pebble |

A flower is a plant.   ⟶   A dog is an | animal |.

| animal | apple | animal | antler | another | animal | ankle | animal |

She is his mother.   ⟶   He is | their | father.

| their | there | these | their | they | their | the | their | three |

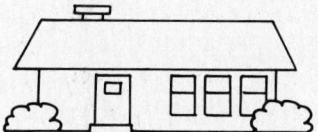 

This is her home.   ⟶   This is her | family |.

| family | funny | family | family | fairy | faintly | family | freshly |

Here are a man and a | woman |.   ⟶   Here are two | women |.

| woman | woman | man | woman | wonder | woman | winner | woolen |
| women | wonder | women | wooden | women | men | women | wander |

Sight Words 1: people, animal, their, family, woman, women

Match these words with the pictures. Write them on the lines.

animals   women   woman   family

_____   _____   _____   _____

Use some of the words below to fill in the blanks.

people	family	animals	child	person	their	animal
women	they	children	men	plants	man	woman

1. Most of her schoolmates are eight- and nine-year-old _____.

2. Trees, grass, shrubs, and flowers are all _____.

3. Grandfather is the oldest man in my _____.

4. Mrs. Swanson is a _____. Mr. Sanchez is a _____.

5. Men, women, and children are all _____.

6. All the children put on _____ boots and scarves.

7. Many people can enter a contest, but just one _____ will win.

8. Hamsters, muskrats, and ostriches are all _____.

9. The seven-year-old _____ likes to see how a magnet attracts nails.

10. Mrs. Holt likes that store because it has so many dresses for _____.

11. My grandfather, father, and uncle are not women; they are all _____.

12. Many people keep some kind of _____ as a pet.

Write the words below in the correct list.

mother
panther
children
lobster
colt
brother

animals

_____

_____

_____

family

_____

_____

_____

Sight Words 1: people, animal, their, family, woman, women

Read the sentences. Circle the word that completes the sentence.

When June grows up, she will be a (child, woman, family).

Many (animals, people, purple) like whipped cream on pumpkin pie.

The bleachers at the game were filled with (footballs, animals, people).

His mother, father, and sister are members of his (brother, family, people).

The mailbox has (they, their, them) address printed on it.

Wayne said the (plants, animals, people) in the garden need watering.

The black panther is a very wild (child, animal, monster).

All of the (woman, child, women) were going to lunch together.

Athletes are (people, animals, tired) who are good in sports.

Our (farther, family, animals) is taking a trip to Vermont in May.

Mrs. Pearson is the name of the (child, man, woman) who gives skating lessons.

The children went home to play under (they, their, them) sprinkler.

Some (hamsters, people, animals) have antlers.

The two (woman, women, children) took their children shopping.

Eight-year-old Jenny is a (woman, man, child).

Some (pant, pumpkin, animal) eats the plants in our garden.

A (man, woman, animal) may be an actress.

Many children put ketchup on (they, them, their) hot dogs.

Dad has to get the muffler fixed on our (father, farther, family) car.

One of the fastest (fish, animals, people) is the ostrich.

They've taken the longest path that leads back to (they, their, them) house.

He was chosen to draw a picture of two (animals, family, people) riding horseback.

Contractions with <u>am</u>, <u>are</u>, <u>is</u>, <u>not</u>, <u>us</u>

Read the first two words and the contraction they make when the words are put together. One letter is left out. Box in the letter that is left out. Write the letter on the line.

w e [a] r e ——→ we're __a__   w h o is ——→ who's ____

t h e y a r e ——→ they're ____   w h a t is ——→ what's ____

I a m ——→ I'm ____   h e r e is ——→ here's ____

l e t u s ——→ let's ____   w h e r e is ——→ where's ____

y o u a r e ——→ you're ____   w e r e n o t ——→ weren't ____

Write the correct contraction for each sentence in the blank.

1. Tell Pete to get his things together because _____ going home.
   where's   we're

2. Queen Eve wants to find out _____ the matter with her throne.
   where's   what's

3. At two o'clock _____ going to see Dr. Chang about your sore throat.
   you're   they're

4. _____ a seat in the front row that's not taken yet.
   We're   Here's

5. Mr. Holt said that _____ going to be the eighth player on the team.
   let's   I'm

6. Dr. Baker took an X-ray of her arm; there _____ any broken bones.
   weren't   where's

7. _____ the kind person who fixed all these things for us?
   Who's   Let's

8. _____ the picture that you had taken yesterday?
   Where's   We're

9. _____ find out where Grandmother put our gifts.
   Let's   I'm

Write the two words that make up each contraction.

you're _____ _____   here's _____ _____   weren't _____ _____

I'm _____ _____   who's _____ _____   what's _____ _____

let's _____ _____   we're _____ _____   they're _____ _____

Contractions with am, are, is, not, us

Cross out the letter that is left out when you put two words together to make a contraction. Then write the contraction on the lines.

you are ⟶ __ __ __'__ __   they are ⟶ __ __ __ __'__ __

we are ⟶ __ __'__ __   what is ⟶ __ __ __ __'__

I am ⟶ __'__   here is ⟶ __ __ __ __'__

let us ⟶ __ __ __'__   where is ⟶ __ __ __ __ __'__

who is ⟶ __ __ __'__   were not ⟶ __ __ __ __ __'__

Write the correct contraction for the two words that are under the first blank. Choose the correct word for the other blank and write it on the line.

1. _____ the tallest slide that we can use on the _____?
   Where is   playground   pretzel

2. _____ the oldest child at this party and I'm having _____.
   I am   fan   fun

3. Put on your woolen cap and mittens and _____ make a _____.
   let us   shovel   snowman

4. There isn't a good seat left for you because _____ _____.
   you are   late   lake

5. _____ a bag of eight of the biggest _____ I can find.
   Here is   apples   please

6. Steve, _____ put all of these sticks together into a _____.
   let us   pole   pile

7. Why _____ you at the _____ yesterday afternoon?
   were not   game   grain

8. _____ going to pick all those peaches when they _____?
   Who is   riding   ripen

9. Didn't you tell me that _____ going on a trip for eight _____?
   they are   dogs   days

Write the contraction for each set of words.

where is _____   I am _____   we are _____

here is _____   you are _____   what is _____

they are _____   let us _____   who is _____

oi   oy

Look at the pictures. Read the sentences that tell about the pictures.
The vowel pairs for you to remember are **oi** and **oy.**

His name is Mike. He is a **boy.**

We plant flowers in **soil.**

Box in oi or oy in these words. Read the words as you box in the vowels.

point   boil   coil   oil   joy

noise   coin   broil   toy   foil

Choose the correct word from above for each picture. Write it neatly on the line.

_____	_____	_____
_____	_____	_____
_____	_____	_____

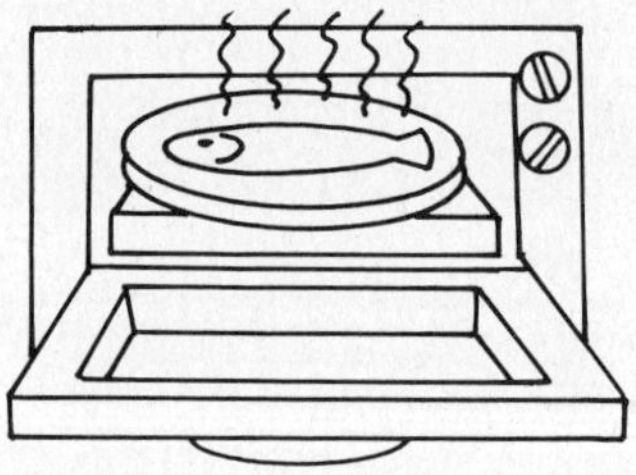

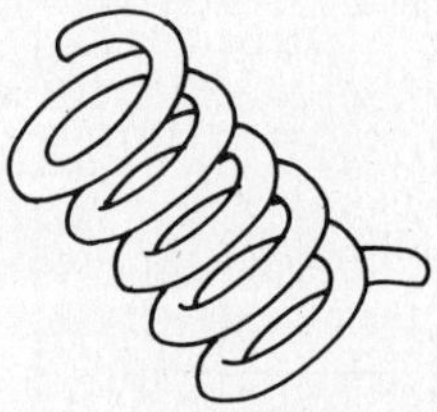

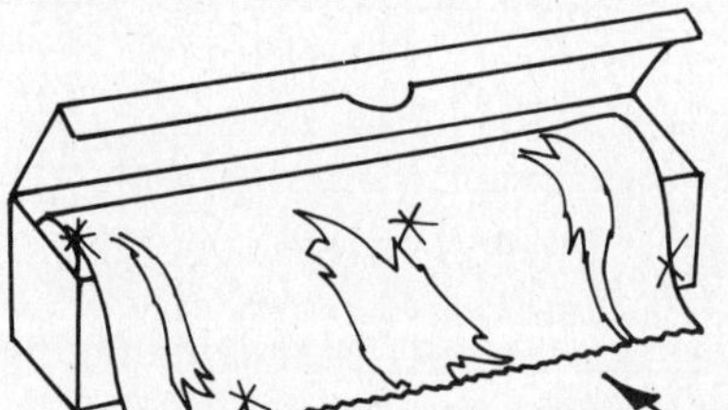

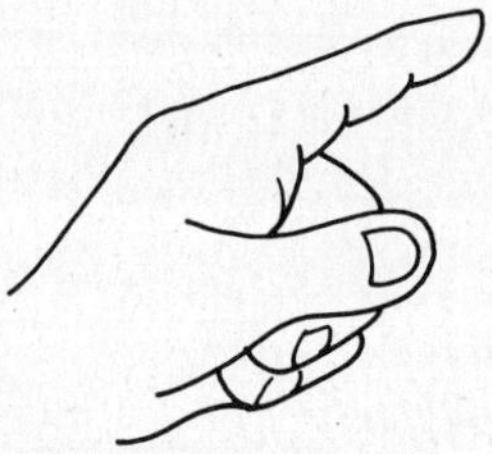

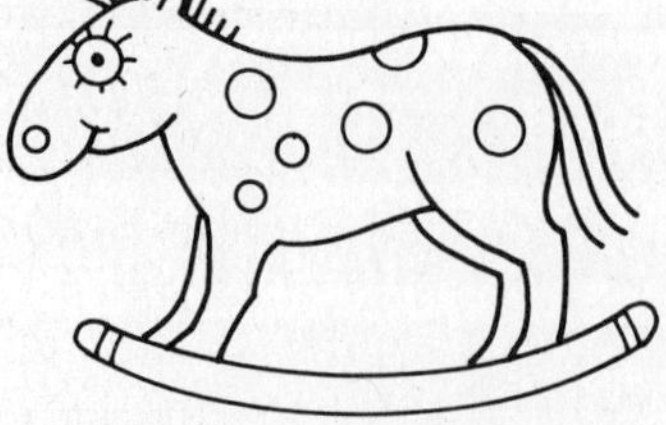

oi   oy

Read the words in each box. Then circle the word that matches the picture.

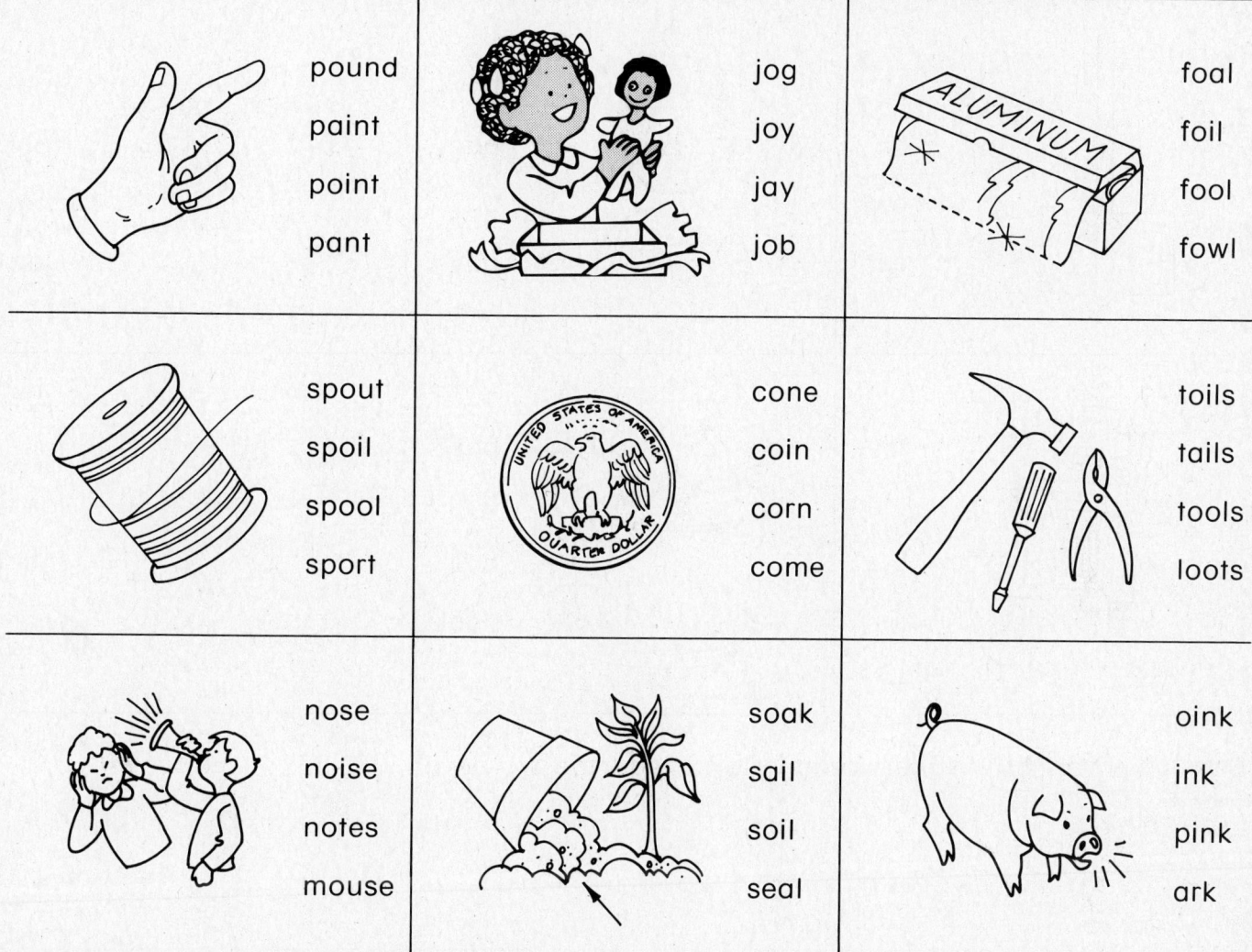

pound	jog
paint	joy
point	jay
pant	job

foal
foil
fool
fowl

spout	cone
spoil	coin
spool	corn
sport	come

toils
tails
tools
loots

nose	soak
noise	sail
notes	soil
mouse	seal

oink
ink
pink
ark

Box in **oi** in the words below. Read the words as you box in the vowels.

coins   noise   points   oink

join   broil   soil

Use the words above to fill in the blanks.

1. A sound that you can hear can be called a _____.

2. A penny, nickel, and dime are all _____.

3. Our teacher explained that in this game you score _____.

4. You plant trees and other plants in _____.

5. We think the sound that a pig makes sounds like "_____."

6. A way to cook meat or fish in the oven is to _____ it.

oi   oy

Read the words in each box. Circle the word that names the picture.

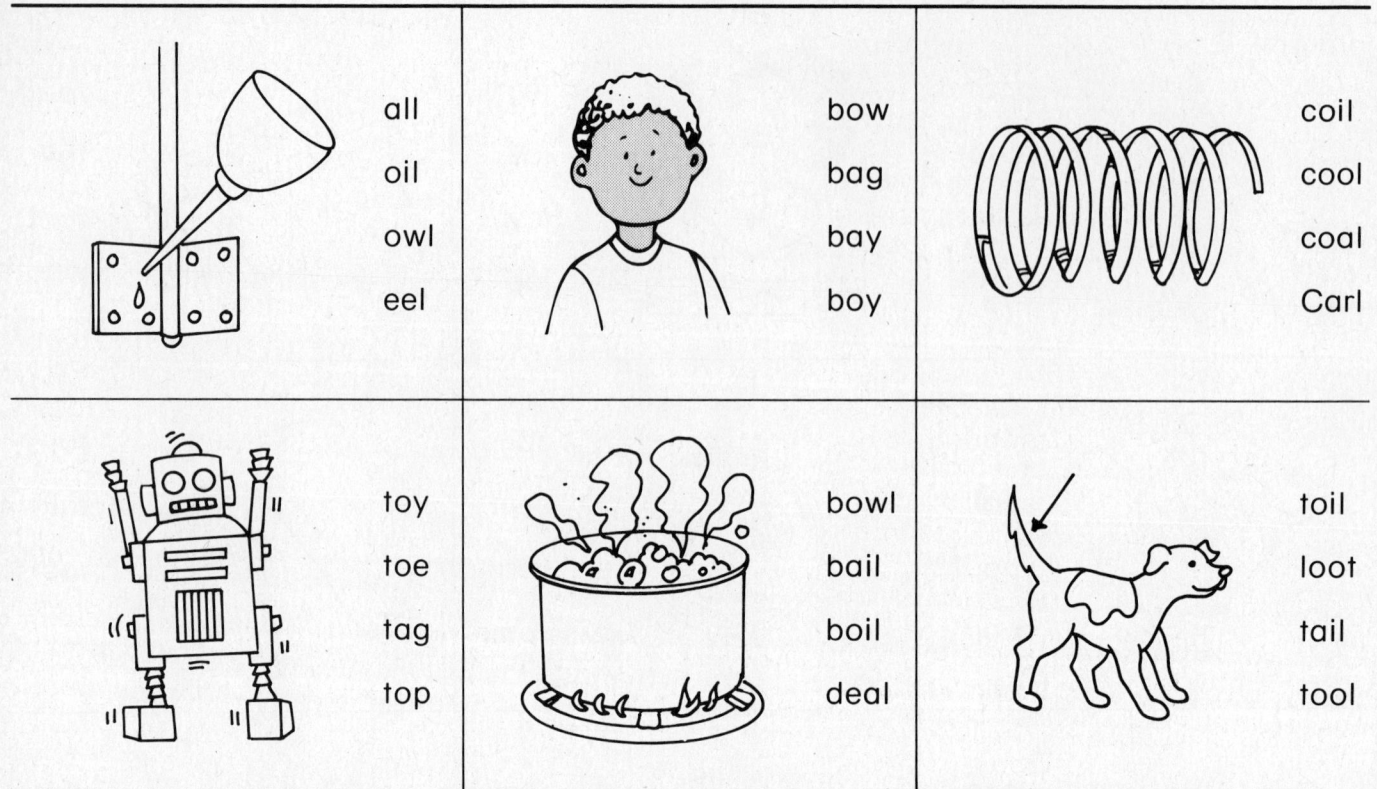

all
oil
owl
eel

bow
bag
bay
boy

coil
cool
coal
Carl

toy
toe
tag
top

bowl
bail
boil
deal

toil
loot
tail
tool

Box in **oi** or **oy** in the words below. Read the words as you box in the vowels.

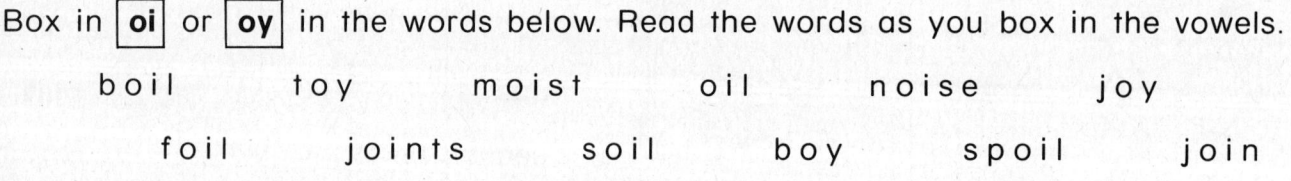

boil   toy   moist   oil   noise   joy

foil   joints   soil   boy   spoil   join

Use the words above to complete these sentences.

1. A child named James is most likely to be a _____.

2. Something that's a little damp or wet is _____.

3. If food isn't kept cold, it will _____.

4. Something that small children play with is a _____.

5. If you cook eggs in hot water, we say that you _____ them.

6. Something that a car needs in order to run is _____.

7. To bring together or connect is to _____.

8. A feeling that is the same as happy or glad is _____.

9. To keep food fresh, you may want to put it into _____.

10. Your elbows and ankles are called _____.

oi   oy

Read the words in each box. Divide them into syllables or word parts that you can say. Keep vowel pairs like **oi, oy, ai,** and **ay** together. Circle the word that matches the picture.

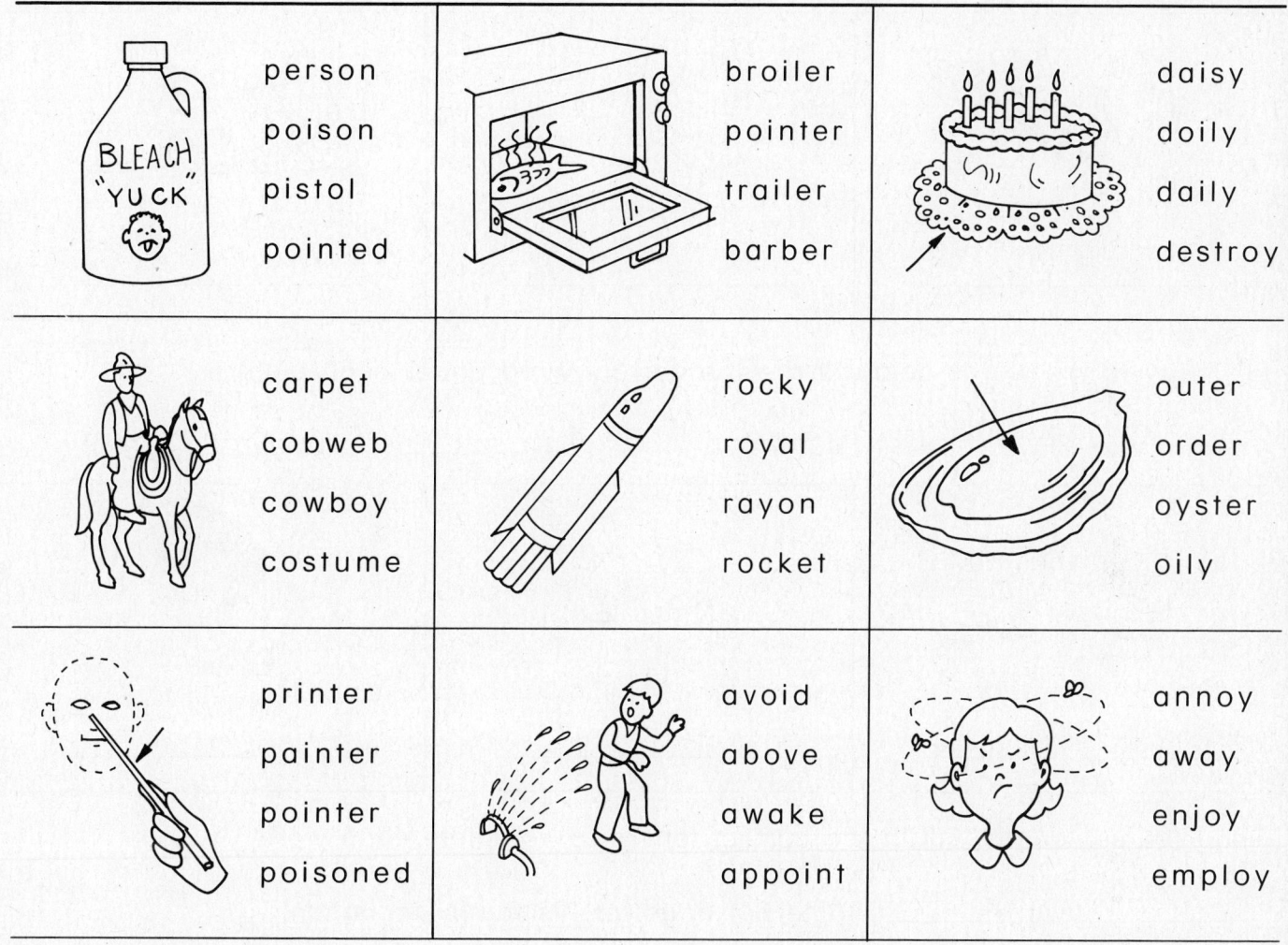

person poison pistol pointed	broiler pointer trailer barber	daisy doily daily destroy
carpet cobweb cowboy costume	rocky royal rayon rocket	outer order oyster oily
printer painter pointer poisoned	avoid above awake appoint	annoy away enjoy employ

Box in | oi | or | oy | in the words below. Read the words as you box in the vowels.

employ   oily   doily   enjoy

royal   appoint   avoid

Use the words above to complete the sentences.

1. When you really like doing something, you _____ it.

2. To give someone a job or to hire a person is to _____ him or her.

3. If something is covered with oil, we say it is _____.

4. Mom put a pretty white _____ on the plate; then she set the cake on it.

5. Things that belong to a king and queen are _____.

6. I hope Mrs. Doyle will _____ me to feed the goldfish this week.

oi   oy

Fill in **oi** in the words below. Write the correct word neatly under each picture.

j __ __ nt   sp __ __ l   s __ __ l   n __ __ se

   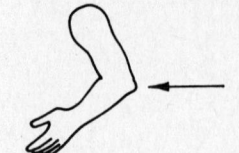   

_____   _____   _____

Fill in **oy** in the words below. Write the correct word under each picture.

b __ __   t __ __   j __ __   J __ __

_____   _____   _____

Read the sentences. Fill in the correct letters to complete each word.

1. B_____ will b_____ some hot dogs for his family for lunch.
    ill   oil   ill   oil

2. Let's tell Tr_____ to bring a tr_____ of crackers and pretzels outside.
         ay oy   ay oy

3. J_____ is the oldest boy in his family and J_____ is his little sister.
  oy oe   oy oe

4. We're putting _____l on that _____d rusty bike to stop it from squeaking.
           ol oi   ol oi

5. Mike p_____nted five silver p_____nts on the stars in his picture.
       oi ai   ai oi

6. S_____k these beans in water before we plant them in the s_____l.
  in oa   oi ai

7. A t_____ is a good t_____ for children to play with.
    op oy   op oy

8. The b_____ is all finished putting his books in his school b_____.
    oy ag   oy ag

oi   oy

Circle the word on the right that will answer the question or complete the sentence.

Who's going to join the Boy Scouts next year?........Joy   Roy   Rags

What do we plant seeds in? ....soil   spring   sail

Which of these can be broiled in the oven? ....meat   hair   met

What do children like to play with? ....tags   toys   stay

Water will begin boiling when it becomes very ....hat   hot   hay

What do we put on an old gate that squeaks? ....owl   oil   low

If we all blow toy horns together, it will sound ....none   nose   noisy

Roping cows on a ranch is a job for a ....copper   cobweb   cowboy

What's an animal that lives in a shell? ....oyster   offer   outer

Where's that loud, noisy "oink" coming from? ....playpen   pens   pigpen

Let's stop here to put gas and oil in the ....jeep   join   jump

When do we see pretty flowers blooming?.............spoil   spring   soil

What do children do with their toys?..................play   ploy   pay

Where can insects be trapped? ....sting   cobweb   cowboy

You can bend your legs and arms wherever you have ...joints   jumps   just

What are nickels and dimes called?...................noise   cones   coins

What is silver colored and comes on a roll?...........fail   foil   folk

Who can have the name Steven? ....boy   bag   bay

What do some snakes have that can harm you? ....person   poison   pointed

What can you use to point to something?.............poison   pointer   pointed

If you like to draw, drawing is something you ....employ   enjoy   avoid

Springs are made of wires that are ....coins   circle   coiled

oi   oy

Read each sentence. Write the correct word in the blanks.

A long time ago my dad used to be a little _____.
boy   bay

Your elbows, ankles, and hips are all called _____.
joints   jumps

They cleaned up their sticky mess with a clean, soapy _____.
Roy   rag

The family really _____ riding their bikes around the block together.
enjoyed   entered

People have two feet, and each foot has five _____.
toys   toes

They're hoping their mom will _____ "yes" next time.
soy   say

My eighteen-year-old brother _____ a bowling team this month.
joined   joked

Dad covered the liver with _____ and put it in the freezer.
fail   foil

Our front gate is old and squeaky. It'll need to be _____.
oiled   owls

Some insects are stuck in that _____ by the front porch.
cobweb   cowboy

Mom and Dad named my little sister _____ and my older brother _____.
Joy   Joe   Joy   Joe

Kathy and Gretchen are sitting together and _____ their hair.
broiling   braiding

Those people weren't at home to shovel the snow off their driveway _____.
today   enjoy

Here's an old rag to wipe your _____ hands when you're done fixing the car.
oily   own

We have to keep the meat frozen so that it will not _____.
spill   spoil

The snake was _____ on the smooth flat rock enjoying the sunshine.
coiled   called

Let's put chicken wire around our garden so our dog can't _____ it.
destroy   dainty

ur

In the words below you see the letter pair **ur** as in <u>pur</u>ple. Use the same sound for **ur** that you use for **er** in teac<u>her</u>. The letter pattern for you to remember is **ur.**

Look at the pictures. Read the sentences that tell about the pictures.

Cats have soft **fur**.

She is a **nurse**.

Box in | ur | in the words below. Read the words as you box in **ur.**

curl   hurt   curd   church   curb

surf   curve   purse   burn   turn

Write the words above neatly on the lines under the correct pictures.

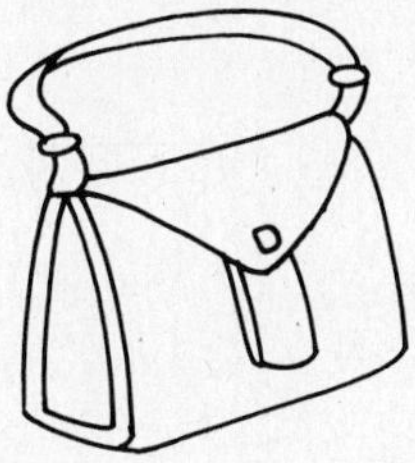

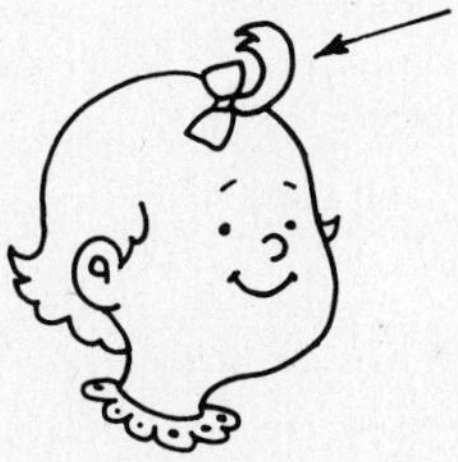

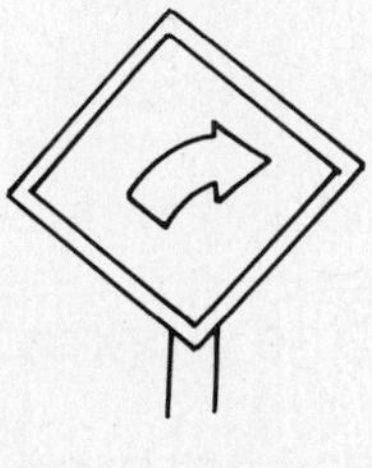

42

ur

Read the words in each box. Circle the word that names the picture.

far / for / **fur** / fun	spare / **spur** / spy / sport	curb / cord / card / **curl**
blur / blue / blow / **burst**	brush / barn / **burnt** / burp	church / curly / chart / **churn**
carve / **curve** / crave / curb	herd / hard / hurdle / **hurt**	turn / **torn** / town / turtle

Box in | ur | in the words below. Read the words as you box in **ur**.

burn   fur   curve   purr

spur   curb   purse

Use the words above to fill in the blanks.

1. Fish are covered with scales. Rabbits have _____.

2. The soft sound a cat makes when it's pleased. _____

3. If food is cooked too long, it may _____.

4. Cars are parked at the side of the street next to the _____.

5. A stiff, sharp point on the legs of a rooster is called a _____.

6. A bend in a road can be called a _____.

ur

Read the words in each box. Divide the words into syllables or word parts that you can say. Keep the letter pair **ur** together. Circle the word that matches the picture.

brunch		hurry		burping	
burden		hurting		burning	
burlap		hurdle		blurry	
burner		hunted		bursting	

turban		stuffy		survive	
turnip		sturdy		surprise	
turtle		stumble		surround	
turnpike		stubborn		surplus	

Box in ur in the words below. Read the words as you box in **ur**.

turnpike   purse   turnip   burner   burp   surprise

pursue   hurry   sturdy   surrounds   survive   turtle

Use the words above to complete these sentences.

1. A wallet, hairbrush, and pen are some things that may be

   in a _____.

2. In many eastern states an expressway is called a _____.

3. When people are in a rush, they're in a _____.

4. Many of my outside plants didn't _____ the very cold winter.

5. Someone or something that's very strong is _____.

6. After an infant drinks, he or she will often _____.

7. Most of its body is covered by its shell. It is a _____.

8. To follow or chase a robber is to _____ him.

9. Do not tell Mom about the gift. It's a _____.

10. That part of the stove that the flame comes from is the _____.

ur

Fill in **ur** in the words below. Then write the correct word neatly under each picture.

b __ __ n   c __ __ ly   t __ __ tle   bl __ __

f __ __   p __ __ sue   h __ __ dle   c __ __ ve

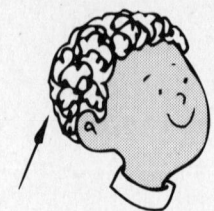

_____

_____

_____

_____

_____

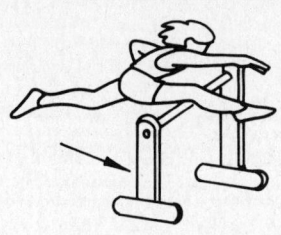

_____

Read the sentences. Fill in the correct letters to complete each word.

1. A fire started in the hay and the b_____n b_____ned down.
                                  ar ur   ar ur

2. Burt h_____t his ankle h_____ting for his lost hamster.
        un ur   un ur

3. The old man c_____ved a swan with a c_____ved neck out of wood.
             ur ar   ur ar

4. The little boy dropped the bag full of baseball c_____ds on the c_____b.
                                    ur ar   ar ur

5. C_____l has a lot of thick c_____ly black hair.
      ur ar   ar ur

6. We're looking f_____ a lost cat with short white f_____.
             or ur   or ur

7. The n_____se will not allow any n_____se in the hall.
      oi ur   ur oi

8. Do not let the t_____tle t_____ble off the steps!
      ur um   ur um

ur

Circle the word that will finish the sentence or answer the question.

What's the noise that water makes when it is going down the drain?

jungle   gurgle   garden   garlic   gamble

What did people use long ago to make milk from their cows into butter?

chins   charms   churches   churns   chimps

What day of the week has the letter pair ur in it?

Monday   turned   Tuesday   Sunday   Thursday

Tennis, racketball, baseball, soccer, and basketball are all

sorts   spurts   spits   sports   stops

The person who cuts and trims the hair of men and boys is a

burlap   borrow   barber   burger   barn

The family across the street has a pet poodle with _____ white hair.

crumble   candle   cuddle   curly   churn

The adults in the family that lives next to us are a grandmother, a mother, and a

furnish   further   father   farther   mother

Animals like raccoons, rabbits, dogs, and hamsters have

from   run   for   fur   far

If you can't see something very clearly, it looks

during   blue   bumpy   blurry   belly

If a big cat chases a little mouse, the mouse will _____ into its hole.

skinny   scour   scurry   sunny   sturdy

If you weren't at school yesterday, you were

absorb   absent   address   avoid   annoy

That boy put too much air into his balloon and it

burst   burn   brush   brisk   bull

ir

In the words below you see the letter pair **ir**. Use the same sound for **ir** that you use for **ur** in <u>purple</u> and **er** in teach<u>er</u>.

Look at the pictures. Read the sentences that tell about the pictures.

Jane is a **girl.**

This is a **bird.**

Box in ir in the words below. Read the words as you box in **ir**.

squirt	dirt	stir	bird	girl
sir	shirt	first	skirt	third

Write the words above neatly on the lines under the correct pictures.

_____ _____ _____

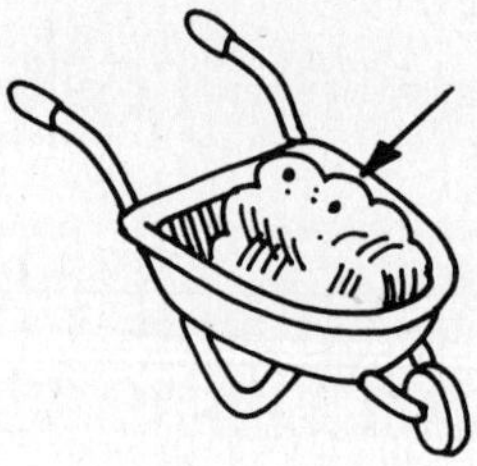

_____ _____ _____

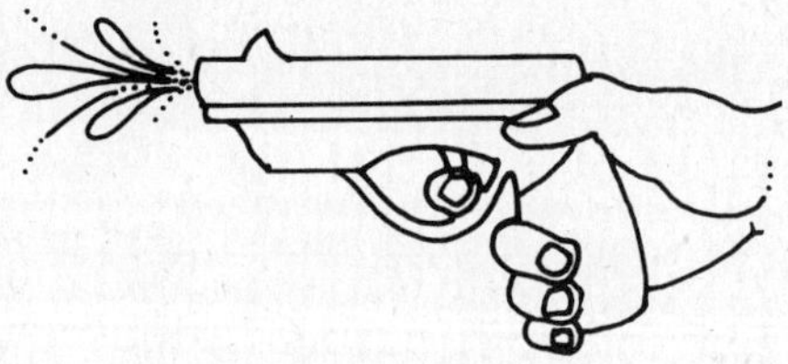

_____ _____ _____

ir

Read the words in each box. Circle the word that matches the picture.

chart short shirt church	fir four far foe	fish fist first foil
purr gill grill girl	fern firm farm form	dart bride bird boil
soar say sir soy	stay store stir star	burnt dart dent dirt

Box in ir in the words below. Read the words as you box in **ir**.

squirm   shirt   bird   third

girl   stir   firm

Use the words above to complete the sentences.

1. If you're number three in line, you are _____.

2. The opposite of boy is _____.

3. This is alive; it has wings, and it can fly. It is a _____.

4. A boy or a girl may put on pants and a _____.

5. To mix with a spoon is to _____.

6. A word that means nearly the same as "hard" is _____.

ir

Read the words in each box. It will help if you divide the longer words into two syllables or word parts that you can say. Circle the word that names the picture.

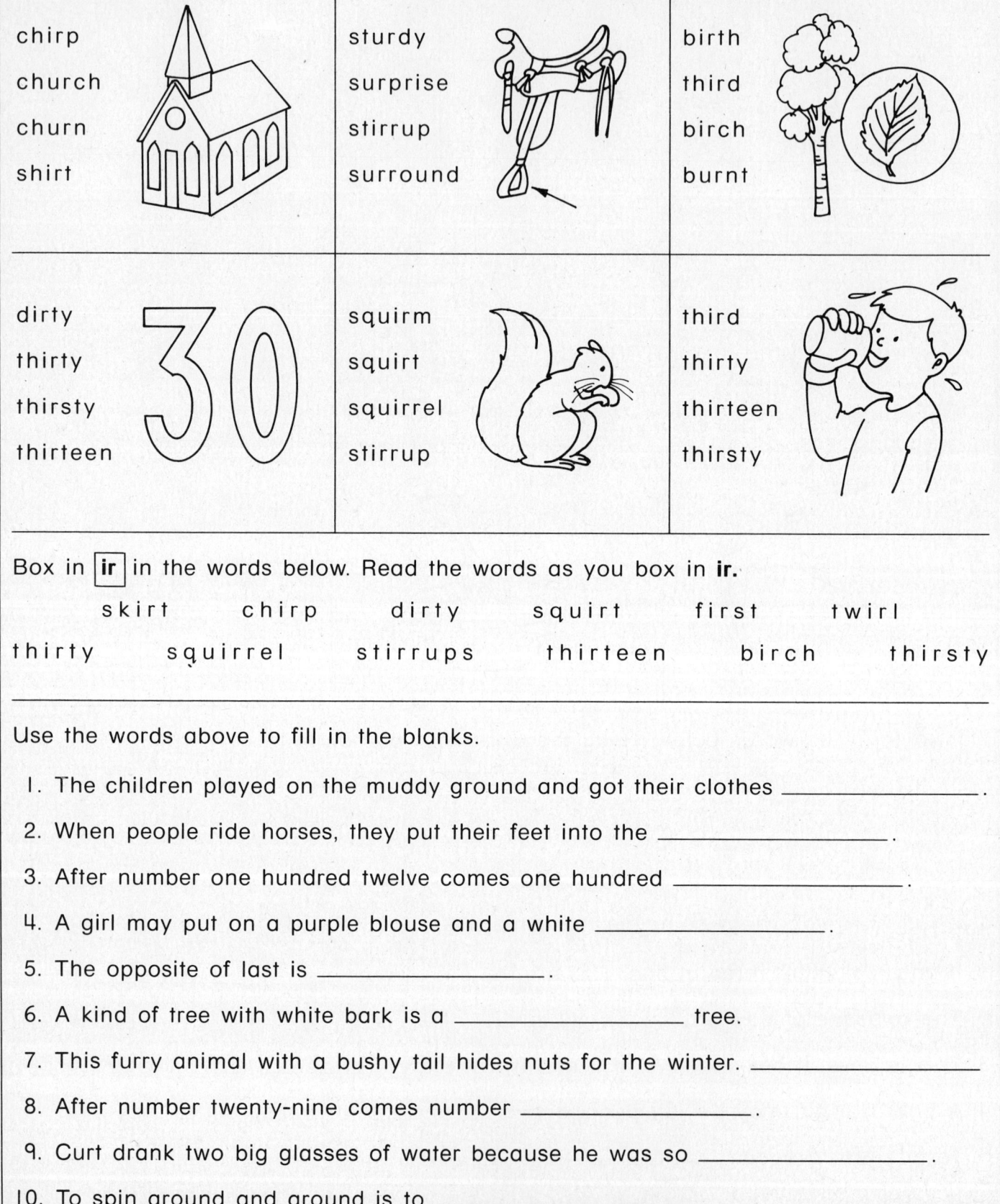

chirp church churn shirt	sturdy surprise stirrup surround	birth third birch burnt
dirty thirty thirsty thirteen	squirm squirt squirrel stirrup	third thirty thirteen thirsty

Box in ir in the words below. Read the words as you box in **ir.**

skirt   chirp   dirty   squirt   first   twirl

thirty   squirrel   stirrups   thirteen   birch   thirsty

Use the words above to fill in the blanks.

1. The children played on the muddy ground and got their clothes _____.

2. When people ride horses, they put their feet into the _____.

3. After number one hundred twelve comes one hundred _____.

4. A girl may put on a purple blouse and a white _____.

5. The opposite of last is _____.

6. A kind of tree with white bark is a _____ tree.

7. This furry animal with a bushy tail hides nuts for the winter. _____

8. After number twenty-nine comes number _____.

9. Curt drank two big glasses of water because he was so _____.

10. To spin around and around is to _____.

ir

Fill in **ir** in the words below. Then write the correct word neatly under each picture.

squ __ __ t   th __ __ teen   sh __ __ t   b __ __ d

f __ __ st   b __ __ thday   th __ __ d   f __ __

_____

_____

_____

_____

_____

_____

Read the sentences. Fill in the correct letters to complete each word.

1. We are looking f_____ a f_____ tree to plant in our front yard.
    ir   or   or   ir

2. Dad wants a blue sh_____t-sleeved sh_____t to go with his dark blue pants.
         or   ir   or   ir

3. Cliff st_____ the gold paint before he paints those st_____.
    ars   irs   irs   ars

4. He ran very f_____st and was the f_____st one to cross the line.
    ir   a   ir   a

5. The d_____t board got all d_____ty while it was stored in our attic.
    ir   ar   ir   ar

6. Jane needs a long flowing sk_____t for the sk_____t she will act in.
                    ir   i   ir   i

7. I was so th_____ty, I felt like drinking th_____ty cans of pop.
    ir   irs   ir   irs

8. Look at those pretty b_____ds flying around by the rose b_____ds.
    ir   u   ir   u

ir

Choose the correct word for each sentence. Write it neatly on the line.

Mom wants my little brother to avoid going near the hot _____.
gift   girl   grill

There are two blue jays _____ in that birch tree.
chirping   chipping   chopping

Boys and girls must never shove to be the _____ in line.
first   fire   farm

Roy has an uncle who grows corn and wheat on his _____.
from   firm   farm

We'll hurry and finish our _____ for Dad before next Thursday.
gift   girl   gill

They need some _____ to tie those twigs together in a bundle.
twirl   twine   twins

The hungry _____ were looking around the woods for nuts.
squints   squirrels   squeals

When cowboys ride horses, they put their feet in the _____.
saddle   stirrups   settlers

Men and women who join the army have to say "Yes, _____" or "Yes, ma'am."
sip   sir   song

Chickens in the barnyard make a lot of noise when they _____.
circle   carve   cackle

We use plastic bottles that _____ ketchup on our hot dogs.
square   squirt   squash

Mrs. Burns wanted to surprise her sister with that _____ purse.
birth   brown   brow

An ostrich is a very big _____ with long sturdy legs.
beetle   bride   bird

Evergreen trees that have cones and leaves like needles are _____ trees.
for   fir   fire

Stirring red paint into white paint makes red and white _____.
swirls   swims   switch

The different colored pinwheels _____ around in the wind.
whirled   wheels   wanted

The _____ have different clothes so people can tell them apart.
twirl   twine   twins

Sight Words 2: both, goes, gone, don't, won't, buy

Read the sentences. Try to read the word in the box. Answer the question or circle the word that completes the next sentence. Below each set of sentences, circle all the words that match the sample word.

They are both reading.

Are they both reading books? _____

Grandfather goes out golfing.

Who goes with him? (Mom, Dave)

both	bath	booth	both	both	birth	bolt	bath	bold
goes	goes	eggs	go	gone	goes	gas	goes	hoes

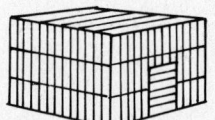

The hamster is gone.

The goldfish (is, isn't) gone.

The class has (goes, gone) home.

The teacher (goes, gone) home, too.

gone	goes	gone	game	glove	gone	go	none	come

It's cold and snowy outside.

Don't forget your (boots, sandals).

He won't eat his lunch.

Will he be hungry soon? _____

don't	dent	done	dot	don't	tent	don't	nod	don't
won't	won't	want	won	won't	wasn't	wool	won't	went

Cats (don't, do) like to get wet.

This cat (will, won't) go out now.

Dad will buy a shirt at this store.

He (won't, will) buy a car here.

buy	boy	bay	buy	bug	buy	due	buy	by

52

Sight Words 2: both, goes, gone, don't, won't, buy

Read the sentences. Write the correct words neatly in the blanks.

going	gone	go	goes	buy	both	won't	don't

1. Troy and Kirk want to go bowling this weekend. They'll _____ go.

2. I have the cash for that wallet. I'll _____ it for myself.

3. I don't think Joy is feeling very well. She _____ eat.

4. Patrick took my corn chips! See, they're all _____ .

5. Uncle Martin fixed my train. It _____ fast again.

6. I wonder where are all those people _____ in such a hurry?

7. Mr. Irving won't buy these woolen gloves. They _____ fit him.

Choose the correct words to fill in the blanks below.

gone	won't	buy	want	goes	both	boy	don't

1. Joey and Roy _____ wanted a turn at bat.

2. The opposite of sell is _____ .

3. A short way to say "do not" is _____ .

4. If someone will not do something, he _____ do it.

5. You and I will go whenever Dad _____ .

6. Kathleen and her family have _____ out to dinner for her birthday.

7. Saturday and Thursday are _____ days of the week.

8. She enjoys swimming so much that she _____ to the pool every week.

9. People who collect rare coins can _____ them in this store.

10. I'm going to buy these earrings for Mom, but _____ tell her.

11. If something is used up, absent, or missing, it is _____ .

12. Those two children won't eat the egg yolk because they _____ like it.

13. Mr. and Mrs. Marshall both _____ to buy that used car.

14. Our teacher said she _____ be finished grading our tests until next week.

Sight Words 2: both, goes, gone, don't, won't, buy

Circle the word that makes sense in the sentence.

Their family has (go, goes, gone) on a month-long trip to Maine.

Troy wants Mom to (sell, buy, both) him a monster costume.

Mom gives away all my old toys that I (do, don't, did) use anymore.

Their family (is, gone, goes) shopping together sometimes.

Give Kirk two dimes so he can (sell, borrow, buy) that little picture book.

Milk (will, do, won't) spoil if it is kept cold.

I won't buy these posters if you (do, don't, did) like them, too.

Each morning at seven o'clock the athlete (go, gone, goes) jogging.

The noisy birds disturbed (them, booth, both) of us.

The kind woman (will, won't, want) let them injure the little kitten.

They're going to a discount store to (borrow, buy, boy) school folders.

We're going to get some cash when we (buy, sell, borrow) our old toys and games.

I hope my little brother (won't, will, do) like the birthday gift I got for him.

That woman gets annoyed (each, none, both) time she hears those noisy dogs.

The squirrel eats the nut and then (go, gone, goes) to hunt for another.

Dad said to hold onto the railing so you (do, dent, don't) stumble on the stairs.

On Thursdays, all of us (goes, gone, go) to lunch at noon.

Most of the people at the party (won't, want, went) want to stay very late.

Mom ordered some apple cobbler for (dessert, lunch, both) of us.

Joy said they've (gone, left, goes) away for thirty days.

Dr. Roy said there was time to see (bath, booth, both) those animals today.

Whose job is it to mow their grass while they're (goes, gone, go)?

Review I

Are all the words listed below the names of animals or people? _____

turtle	puppy	panther	horse
calf	squirrel	owl	lobster
chicken	eagle	kitten	hamster
snail	crow	seagull	crab
rabbit	blue jay	ostrich	goldfish

List six animals from the ones listed above that have fur.

_____   _____   _____

_____   _____   _____

Which of the animals in the list above have shells?

_____   _____   _____

_____   _____   _____

Which of the animals do people most often keep as pets?

_____   _____   _____

_____   _____   _____

List all the birds below.

_____   _____   _____

_____   _____   _____

Use these animal words to complete each sentence below.

dog   horses   turtles   blue jays   kitten   squirrels   ostrich

1. The cowboys have gone riding on their big white _____ .

2. The woman who lives next to us has a _____ that likes to dig in the dirt.

3. Please don't go near that nest of _____ in our birch tree.

4. That little girl gave her _____ its first bowl of milk.

5. The bird that has the strongest legs is an _____ .

6. The furry gray _____ are hiding their nuts in our yard.

7. I'll buy a tank and put stones and shallow water in it for both _____ .

Review I

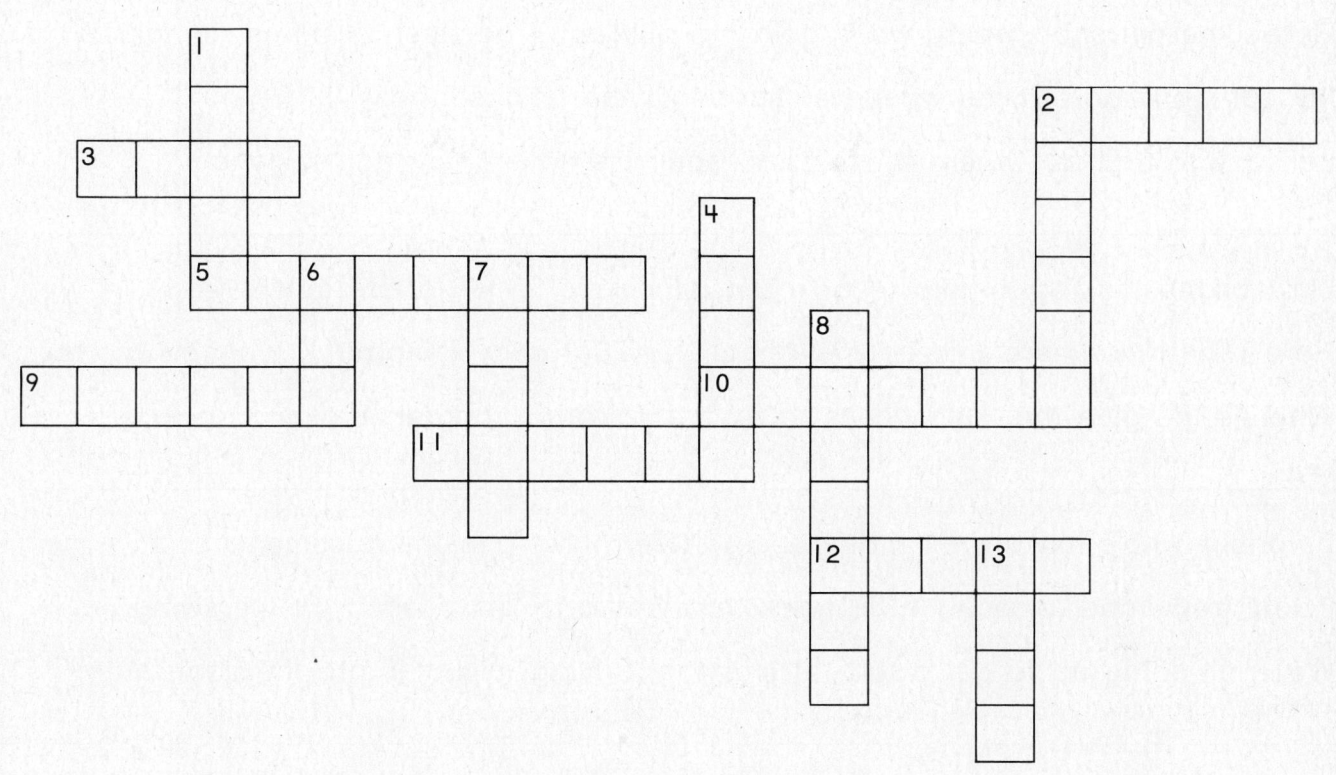

Find the words that will complete the sentences below. Print the words neatly into the crossword puzzle.

| animals | poison | woman | hurt | girls | purse | toys |
| kingdom | annoy | subtract | boy | points | family | dirty |

Across

2. A woman may buy this.

3. If you're injured, you're ____ .

5. You do this in math class.

9. There are four people in his ____ .

10. You see these at the zoo.

11. You must never taste or swallow this.

12. You need a bath when you're ____ .

Down

1. Joy and Holly are both ____ .

2. You count these to keep score.

4. Mrs. Burton is a ____ .

6. Roy is a ____ .

7. This means to bother someone.

8. A king rules his ____ .

13. Children play with these.

Review I

Read the sentences. Circle the word that completes each sentence.

Here's the pet shop where we're going to buy our (hamster, hundred, hungry).

My cat won't go outside whenever I'm using the (house, hose, hurt).

Let's try to find out where those frisky squirrels have (got, game, gone).

I'm (biking, baking, broiling) a frozen peach pie for an after-dinner treat.

Here's the rink where Sue goes skating every Saturday (morning, Monday, month).

Where's the glue that Dad needs to fix the (brother, border, broken) toy?

I wonder who's making all that (nose, noise, nurse) in the basement.

I don't remember whose (turn, truck, torn) it is to get pushed on the swing.

We're all lining up to get a turn at (drying, driving, diving) into the pool.

What's he doing with that big (empty, plenty, employ) cardboard box?

Where's Roy going to put all those (trays, turnips, toys) he got for his birthday?

Mom said we weren't going to see Dr. Baker until (from, four, first) o'clock.

Today we're both going to be carving (scary, stay, sorry) jack-o'-lanterns.

Ernest won't drive on the expressway when there's a lot of (trains, tickets, traffic).

I'll take the rolls out of the oven when the (thinner, timer, third) goes off.

Read the words below. Write them into the list if they belong.

One-Syllable Words		Two-Syllable Words	
nurse	_____	employ	_____
appoint		squirt	
oyster	_____	dimple	_____
broil		cowboy	
points	_____	target	_____
toys		geese	

Words with one middle consonant (closed syllable)

Many words have one consonant in the middle. If you divide the words after the middle consonant, you have a syllable with the CONSONANT-VOWEL-CONSONANT pattern like this: wagon → wag·on. This is called a closed syllable. Read that syllable just like a short vowel word.

Circle the first syllable of each word. Include the middle consonant. Read the two syllables together. Write the whole word below the correct picture.

camel	ravel	gravel	lemon	second
dragon	salad	medal	petal	desert
limit	cabin	Saturn	present	record

_____ _____ _____

_____ _____ _____

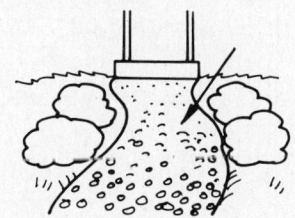  

_____ _____ _____

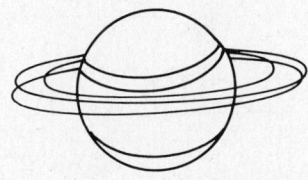  

_____ _____ _____

Words with one middle consonant (closed syllable)

Divide the words into syllables and write them on the lines. Then circle the correct word for each picture.

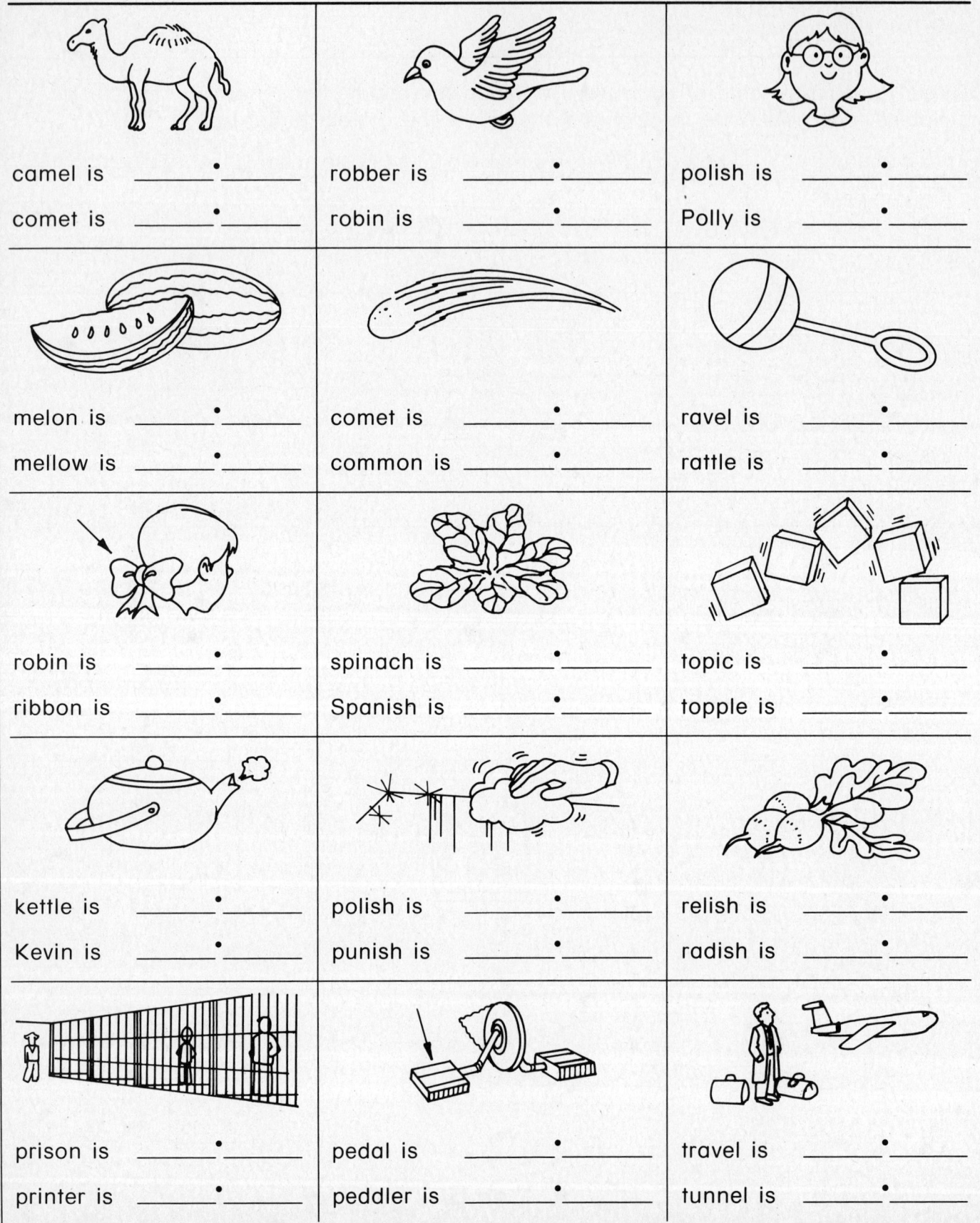

camel is _____ • _____

comet is _____ • _____

robber is _____ • _____

robin is _____ • _____

polish is _____ • _____

Polly is _____ • _____

melon is _____ • _____

mellow is _____ • _____

comet is _____ • _____

common is _____ • _____

ravel is _____ • _____

rattle is _____ • _____

robin is _____ • _____

ribbon is _____ • _____

spinach is _____ • _____

Spanish is _____ • _____

topic is _____ • _____

topple is _____ • _____

kettle is _____ • _____

Kevin is _____ • _____

polish is _____ • _____

punish is _____ • _____

relish is _____ • _____

radish is _____ • _____

prison is _____ • _____

printer is _____ • _____

pedal is _____ • _____

peddler is _____ • _____

travel is _____ • _____

tunnel is _____ • _____

Words with one middle consonant (closed syllable)

Divide the longer words into syllables. Write them in the correct blanks. One word in each group will be used two times.

A book may have many of these. _____	chatter
People can pray at a _____.	chapters
There are more pages than _____ in a book.	chopping
	chapel

Timmy wants Dad to buy that red _____ with the white wheels.	wiggle
Look at their brown and white dog _____ its tail.	Wagner
Years ago a farmer who didn't have a truck used a horse and	wagging
_____.	wagon

Both women are _____ that big sack of dirt to the garden.	dragon
In fairy tales we sometimes read about a fire-breathing _____.	drapes
A _____ is not a real animal.	dragging
	dagger

Alex has finished nailing that _____ of wood onto the wall.	panel
Saturn has rings around it; it is the second biggest _____.	pansy
We're going to _____ our den next Saturday.	panther
	planet

I won't have to dust and _____ the dining room chairs today.	pollen
The woman who lives across the street is named _____.	pots
Let's see if that big bird can say, "_____ wants a cracker!"	Polly
	polish

Mrs. Boyer cut up a _____ for us to eat as a snack.	mellow
The _____ tasted very sweet and ripe.	Melvin
There's a boy named _____ in my English class.	melon
	mattress

Our family goes to one of these _____ in the woods each fall.	cabins
Arthur is drawing a picture of a _____ riding his horse.	cabs
We enjoy visiting the log _____ the pilgrims made years ago.	cowboy
	cobweb

60

Adding -y to words that end with e

You remember that the vowel-consonant-vowel pattern in a word tells you to use the vowel name when you read the word, like this: sh⎡ade⎦. In the words on this page, **y** is a vowel. Then the vowel-consonant-vowel pattern looks like this: sh⎡ady⎦.

Box in the vowel-consonant-vowel pattern if you see it in the words below.
Read all the words.

b o n y   b u n n y   s c a l y   w h i n y

s l i m y   s k i n n y   s c a r y   n o s y   s u n n y

Write the words that have a vowel-consonant-vowel pattern in the blanks beside the base words they came from.

whine _____   scare _____   slime _____

bone _____   nose _____   scale _____

When you add **-y** to words that end with e, take off the e and add y. In this way you keep the vowel-consonant-vowel pattern.   scare + y → scare̸ → scary

Add **-y** to these words. Write the words you make on the lines.

shake̸ _____   stone _____   shade _____

wave _____   shine _____   scare _____

smoke _____   flake _____   bone _____

To find the base word: 1. Take off the **y**.   2. Then add e.   shady̸ → shade

rosy _____   stony _____   wavy _____

shiny _____   hazy _____   smoky _____

shaky _____   flaky _____   shady _____

Read both sentences. Find one word in the first sentence that you can add **y** to. Use the word you make to complete the second sentence. Write it in the blank.

1. That costume may <u>scare</u> her.

   It's a _____ costume.

2. There's so much smoke in that room.

   It's a _____ room.

3. Some animals are covered with scales.

   These animals are _____.

4. We'll wax our car so it'll shine.

   We want our car to be _____.

5. That path has many stones.

   It's a _____ path.

6. Her cheeks are rose colored.

   She has _____ cheeks.

Adding -y to words that end with e

Circle the words below that have vowels that say their name. Then use the words to complete the sentences.

whiny	crispy	shady	scaly	misty	shiny
sticky	wavy	bony	smoky	stony	skinny
shaky	rosy	bunny	rusty	foggy	flaky

1. There's a lot of shade in our yard.

   We've got a _____ yard.

2. My hair has many waves in it.

   I've got _____ hair.

3. This desk shakes when I write on it.

   It is a _____ desk.

4. Some fish you eat have many bones.

   I don't like such _____ fish.

Answer the questions with yes or no.

1. Are some animals scary? _____
2. Can a beach be stony? _____
3. Can a lake be wavy? _____
4. Can a pie crust be flaky? _____
5. Are some coins shiny? _____
6. Are people scaly? _____
7. Can a ladder be shaky? _____
8. Is a pumpkin bony? _____

Choose the correct word for each sentence. Write it on the line.

He _____ because he had just seven points and I had eight. I'm going to let my dog in because I hear him _____ outside.	whined whining whiny
My brother says that fish and snakes are covered with _____. We can't cook the fish before we finish _____ them.	scaling scales scaly
That child loves being outside when the sun is _____. Let's polish the tarnished silverware so it will look _____.	shiny shine shining
Here's some more water to put out that _____ campfire. Where's all that _____ coming from?	smoke smoky smoked

62

Adding -est to words that end with e

To add **-est**:   I. Take off the e.   2. Add **-est**.   3. Write the word.

safe + est → safe̷ → safest   This way you keep the <u>vowel-consonant-vowel</u> pattern.

safe _____   close _____   ripe _____

wide _____   stale _____   rare _____

To find the <u>base word</u>:   I. Take off **est**.   2. Add e.   3. Write the word.

    cute̷st → cute

safest _____   bravest _____   finest _____

widest _____   tamest _____   rudest _____

Choose the word that belongs in each sentence. Write it on the line.

Mom said to remember that the pool _____ at four o'clock today.	closest
We pulled off the road to ask where's the _____ drugstore.	closed closes
The sentence told us to circle the _____ animal in the picture.	tamer
The wild colt is being _____ by a very skilled trainer.	tamest tamed
Helen says that a life jacket is much _____ than an inner tube.	safest
Our teacher told us which is the _____ exit to use in case of fire.	safer safe
Here's the store where Dad buys the _____ baked goods.	fines
My borrowed book was past due, so I was _____ a dime.	fined finest

---

Circle the words below that have vowels that say their name.

quickest   stalest   sharpest   safest   softest   fastest

wisest   hottest   bravest   widest   tamest   finest

Find the base words. Write them on the lines.

slimy _____   rarest _____   palest _____   whiny _____

rudest _____   grimy _____   closest _____   wisest _____

-ar that you read like -er

Often when a word has **ar** in the <u>second syllable</u>, it <u>sounds</u> different from the **ar** in <u>car</u>. It sounds like **er** in <u>teacher</u>.

Look at the pictures. Read the sentences that tell about each picture. Circle the word that will make the second sentence true.

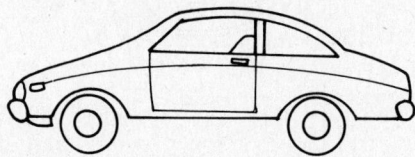

This is a **car.**

<u>Car</u> is a (one, two) syllable word.

This is a **dollar.**

<u>Dollar</u> is a (one, two) syllable word.

Box in ⬚**ar** in the words below. Read the words as you box in **ar**.

lizard   collar   wizard   buzzard   backward

hazard   blizzard   mustard   orchard   burglar

Choose the correct word from above for each picture. Write it neatly on the line.

_____

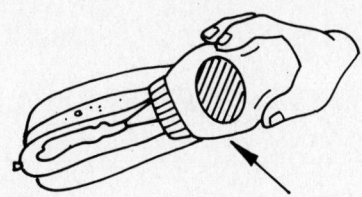

_____

_____

_____

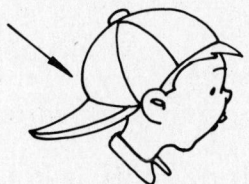

_____

_____

_____

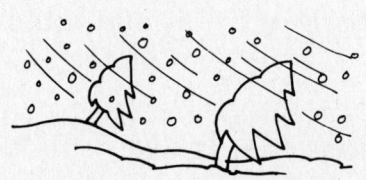

_____

_____

-ar that you read like -er

Read all the words. Circle the word that names the picture.

pillow
player
pillar
pilgrim

backfire
backyard
backwoods
backward

custard
costume
crisper
custom

calling
caller
dollar
collar

buzzard
buzzer
dusty
busses

forecast
frosted
forest
forward

Box in ar in the words below. Read the words as you box in the letters.

wizard   collar   pillar   buzzard   blizzard

lizard   orchard   hazard   custard   nectar

Use the words above to fill in the blanks.

1. A tall post often made of stone that is used to support a roof

   is a _____ .

2. A fairy-tale person with hidden powers who casts spells is a _____ .

3. A big snowstorm with strong winds and blowing snow is a _____ .

4. A big, strong bird that eats small animals is a _____ .

5. That part of a shirt or jacket that goes around your neck is a _____ .

6. A sweet drink inside flowers that hummingbirds and bees like. _____

7. A kind of reptile that has legs and a tail and is covered with dry scaly skin.

   _____

8. A sweet blend of milk and eggs that is like a pudding is a _____

9. Many apple trees planted in long neat rows is an apple _____ .

10. Something that is a risk or that can harm you is a _____ .

-or that you read like -er

Often when a word has **or** in the second syllable, it <u>sounds</u> different from the **or** in <u>cor</u>n. It sounds like **er** in <u>teach**er**</u>.

Look at the pictures. Read the sentences that tell about each picture. Circle the word that will make the second sentence correct.

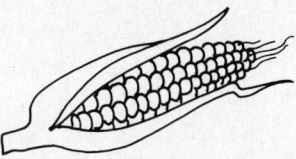

This is **corn.**

<u>Corn</u> is a (one, two) syllable word.

But this is **doctor.**

<u>Doctor</u> is a (two, one) syllable word.

Box in or in the words below. Read the words as you box in **or**.

harbor   armor   color   tractor   sailor

doctor   record   stubborn   mayor   actor

Choose the correct word from above for each picture. Write it neatly on the line.

-or that you read like -er

Read all the words. Circle the word that names the picture.

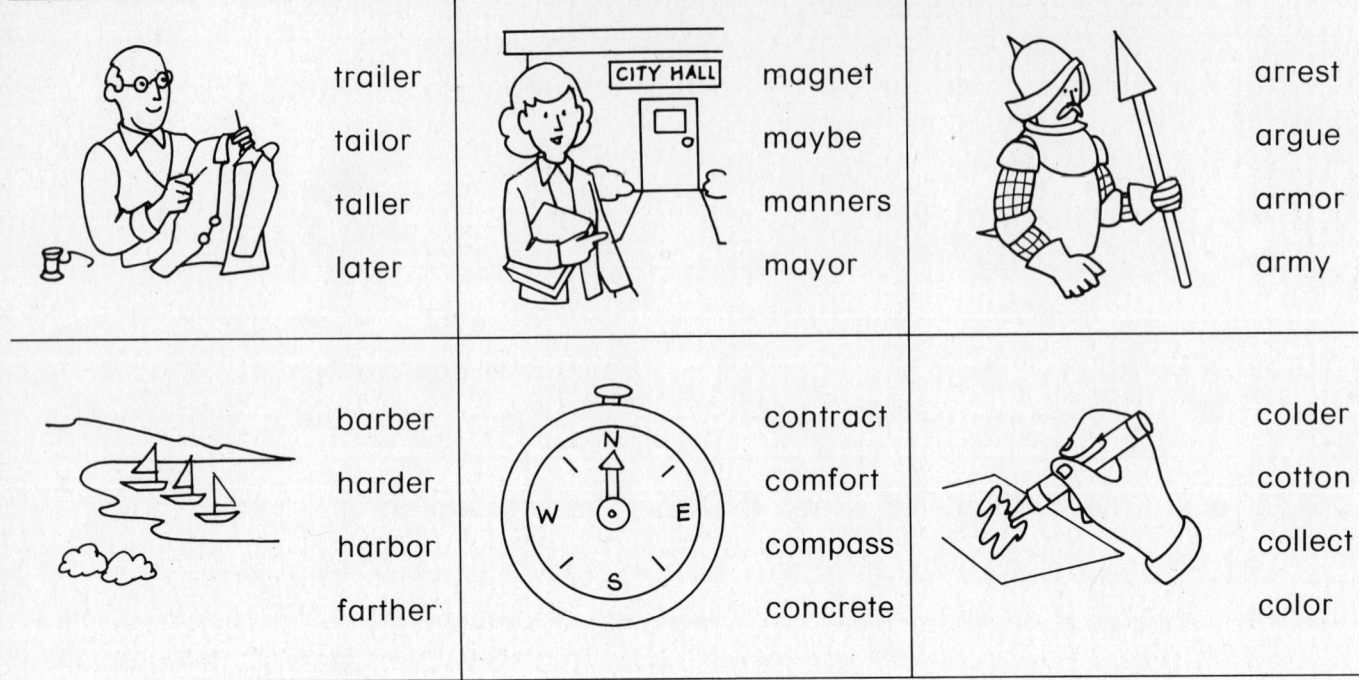

	trailer		magnet		arrest
	tailor		maybe		argue
	taller		manners		armor
	later		mayor		army

	barber		contract		colder
	harder		comfort		cotton
	harbor		compass		collect
	farther		concrete		color

Box in | or | in the words below. Read the words as you box in the letters.

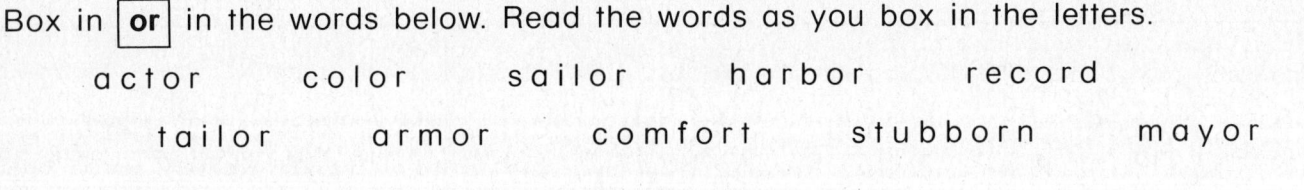

actor   color   sailor   harbor   record

tailor   armor   comfort   stubborn   mayor

Use the words above to complete the sentences.

1. A person who works on a ship on the sea is a _____.

2. Long, long ago men in battle covered themselves with metal _____.

3. To make a person who is sad or upset feel better is to

    _____ him or her.

4. Someone whose job it is to make or fix clothes is a _____.

5. We gave him many reasons, but he still won't join us. He's being

    _____.

6. The part of a sea, lake, or river that is safe from storms is a _____.

7. A person who performs in a play is called an _____.

8. A flat, round disc with grooves that you play to hear songs is a _____.

9. Yesterday, the people of this town chose Mr. Roberts as their _____.

10. I didn't like that shade of red nail polish. I want a different _____.

-or that you read like -er

Here are some more words in which the **or** sounds like the **er** in teach<u>er</u>.

Box in $\boxed{\text{or}}$ in the words below. Read the words as you box in **or**.

worst   words   workbench   world   work   worm   workbook

Write the words above neatly under the correct pictures.

robin nurse stir point	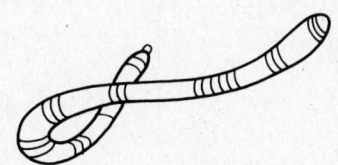	
_____	_____	_____

_____	_____	_____

Use these words to complete the sentences below.

worst   worry   worms   worthwhile   worth   worthy
working   worse   worship   workbench   world   words

1. I'm reading a gardening book that says _____ are good for the soil.

2. One lane of the expressway is closed because men are _____ on it.

3. We're taking our dog to get a shot so we won't _____ about him getting sick.

4. One dollar is _____ ten dimes.

5. The globe is a model of the _____.

6. Take these nuts and bolts and put them in the box on the _____.

7. I'll stay home and rest today so my cold won't get any _____.

8. The blizzard last winter was the _____ one in thirty years.

9. All that studying I did was _____ because I passed my math test.

10. Many people go to churches or temples to _____.

Soft c   -ce

All of the words on this page end with **ce**. The **ce** pattern tells you to use the s̲ sound for the c̲. The c̲ that sounds like s̲ is called **soft c̲**.

Look at the pictures. Read the sentence that tells about each picture.

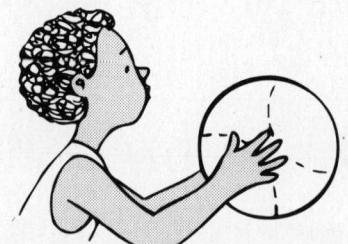

He will **bounce** the ball.

He is a **prince.**

Box in ce in the words below. Read the words as you box in **ce**.

prince   dance   bounce   ounce   prance

glance   fence   pounce   Vince   chance

Look at the pictures. Write the correct word from above under each picture.

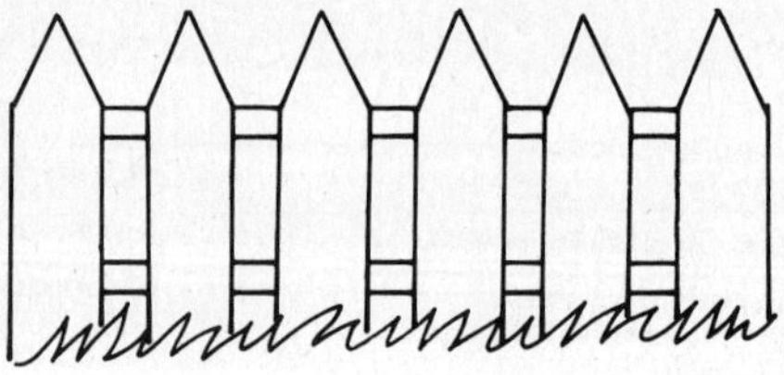

_____   _____   _____

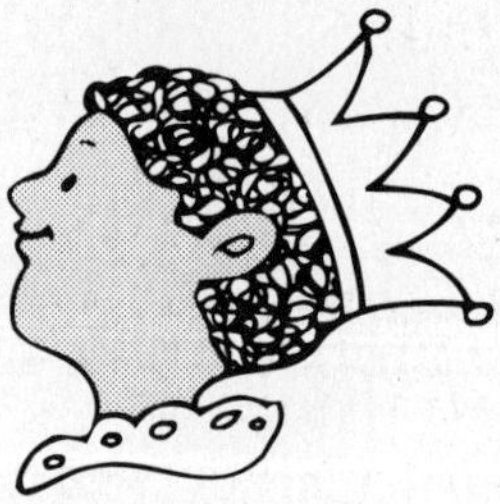

_____   _____   _____

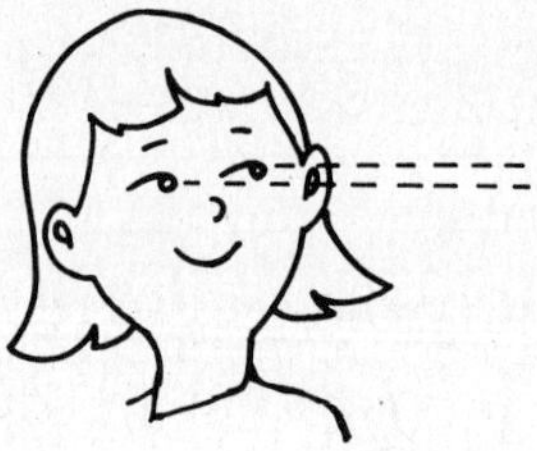

_____   _____   _____

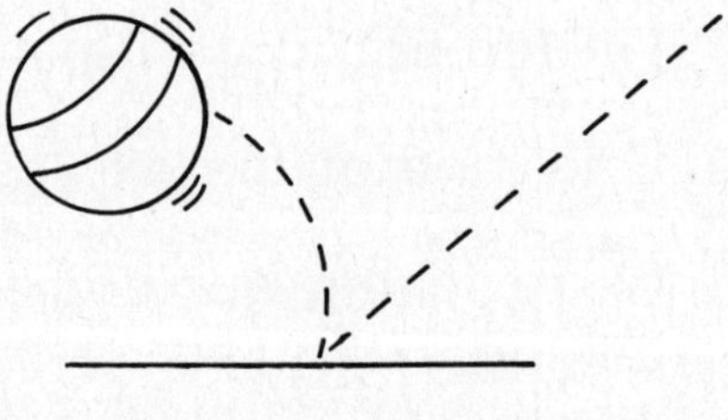

Soft c   –ce

Read the words in each box. Circle the word that matches the picture.

damp / banks / dance / drags	glands / glance / glass / clamps	slips / sick / since / sinks
prowl / branch / pranks / prance	bench / French / fence / first	ounce / ouch / ours / orange
bounce / bunks / bound / hound	claims / chase / chance / cranks	pouch / pound / pounce / punch

Box in [ce] in the words below. Read the words as you box in **ce**.

ounces   prince   glance   fence

prance   pounce   dance

Use the words above to fill in the blanks.

1. People at a party often like to do this. _____

2. This may be made of wood or metal to surround a yard. _____

3. To leap or spring at a person or animal is to _____.

4. To look at something very quickly is to _____ at it.

5. A good trainer can teach most horses to _____.

6. Sixteen of these make one pound. _____

Soft c   -ce

Fill in **ce** in the words below. Read the words as you fill in **ce**. Then write the correct word neatly under each picture.

prin __ __   dan __ __   glan __ __   boun __ __

fen __ __   oun __ __   pran __ __   poun __ __

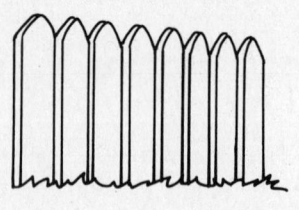

_____

_____

_____

_____

_____

_____

Read the sentences. Fill in the correct letters to complete each word.

1. Vince shouted "ou_____" when that sixteen-ou_____ bottle fell on his toe.
                     nce   ch   ch   nce

2. The black p_____ p_____ on something in the tall grass.
                    anther   ounced   anther   ounced

3. That basketball player hasn't scored a s_____ point s_____ the game started.
                                ince   ingle   ince   ingle

4. The ball rolled out of boun_____ after it boun_____ off his mitt.
                         ced   ds   ced   ds

5. She was gl_____ that she gl_____ at the clock just in time.
                  ad   anced   ad   anced

6. The pr_____ white horses will pr_____ at the front of the parade.
                ance   etty   ance   etty

7. The women had a ch_____ to ch_____ while they waited in line.
                  at   ance   ance   at

8. The puppy had to jump the f_____ to f_____ the ball.
                  ence   etch   ence   etch

Soft c   -ce

Choose the correct word for each sentence. Write it neatly on the line.

The saleswoman sold our family _____ chairs for the kitchen

Waves slammed against the dock with such _____ that it shook.

To keep snow from drifting onto the road, men put up snow_____.

force
four
fences
forks

It was hard for me to make a _____ between cake or custard pie.

I'll _____ the ripest apples when we go the apple orchard.

We both have a _____ to win first prize in the baking contest.

choice
coin
chance
choose

Mr. Gordon got most of the _____ for mayor.

When people talk or sing or shout, they use their _____.

I hope all this noise _____ disturb your family.

Vince
voices
votes
won't

I wonder whose stuffed animal little _____ is playing with.

I don't think buying that squirt gun was a good _____.

Mr. and Mrs. Adams won't mind if their son _____ that club.

joins
Joyce
choice
voice

The _____ were picked too soon and they weren't ripe yet.

After the battles ended, there was _____ in the land again.

Their pet cat often _____ on that toy rubber mouse.

pounces
peace
peaches
peaks

If Joy goes skating today without gloves and a hat, she'll _____.

A shepherd is someone whose work is to take care of a _____
of sheep.

The wool that covers the body of a sheep is called _____.

fleece
freeze
fence
flock

Many old folk tales begin with "_____ upon a time."

To do something one time is to do it _____.

My birthday present from my uncle was a one-_____ gold coin.

one
out
ounce
once
(wunce)

© 1995 SRA/McGraw-Hill

Soft c   -ce

Use the words below to fill in the blanks in the sentences.

France	distance	pounce	fence	absence
ounce	sentences	balance	entrance	bounces

1. The wild panther may _____ on another animal.

2. They'll park their car close to the _____ to the zoo.

3. At school we're given eight-_____ cartons of milk for lunch.

4. We say she's French because she and her family were born in _____.

5. The _____ to the town where my uncle Floyd works is thirty miles.

6. Mrs. Baldwin asked me to correct spelling mistakes in four _____.

7. Vince sometimes _____ his basketball as he walks down the street.

8. After being gone from school, we must bring a note to explain

   our _____.

9. The silly clown lost his _____ and fell backward onto the ground.

---

convince	force	announced	dances	Greece
enforce	chance	advance	peace	since

1. The Greek woman has gone on a trip to visit her family in _____.

2. Mrs. Kirk is teaching us some easy folk _____ from
   around the world.

3. The saleswoman won't _____ Mom to buy both the purse
   and the skirt.

4. Justin hasn't seen Dr. Quinn _____ last winter.

5. The people waited until someone _____ the winner of the contest.

6. Arthur thinks that he may want to join the air _____
   when he grows up.

7. Mr. Monroe gave Robert a second _____ to solve that math problem.

8. Teachers on the playground help to _____ rules for playing safely.

9. Our class wasn't told in _____ about the quiz today.

Soft c̲ **ce- ci-**

1. On this page are words that have the letter pair **ce** at the beginning of the word. You do the same as you did when **ce** was at the end. Use the soft sound of c̲.
2. In some words you see the letter pair **ci**. The rule is the same as for **ce**: Use the soft sound of c̲ when you see **ci.**
3. Since e̲ and i̲ are the vowels in these words, you must say their sounds.

A penny is one **cent.**

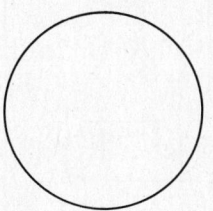

This is a **circle.**

Box in ce or ci in the words below. Read the words. Then write them neatly on the lines below the correct pictures.

circle   cent   center   circus   city   cell   cement

_____

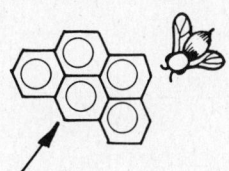

_____

_____

_____

_____

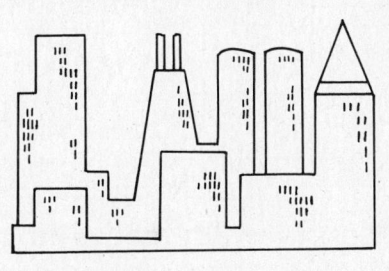

_____

Find all the words that <u>do not</u> have <u>soft c.</u> Draw a circle around them.
Read all the words.

cent	call	center	cup	contest	can't
come	cell	counter	curly	costume	candy

Soft c   ce-   ci-

Read the words in each box. Divide the longer words into syllables or word parts that you can say. Keep the letter pairs **ce** or **ci** together. Circle the word that matches the picture.

kitty	kill	canvas
cry	cell	circus
city	call	campus
silly	colt	circle
cent	cent	curly
cell	Kent	circle
cold	can't	crinkle
call	center	circus
circle	contest	counter
curl	central	center
cry	contract	central
circus	center	cent

Box in **ce** or **ci** in the words below. Read the words as you box in the letters.

circus   circle   cells   cents

cement   city   center

Use the words above to complete the sentences.

1. The queen bee lays her eggs in _____ made of beeswax.

2. You may see clowns doing stunts at a _____.

3. Two nickels are worth ten _____.

4. A round shape that has no corners is a _____.

5. Another word for "middle" can be _____.

6. Concrete for sidewalks and driveways is made with _____.

Soft c   ce-   ci-

Fill in **ce** in the words below. Write the correct word on the line under the pictures.

    __ __ nt   __ __ ment   __ __ ll   __ __ nter

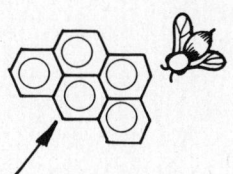      

_____   _____   _____

Fill in **ci** and write the correct word under the pictures.

    __ __ rcle   __ __ ty   __ __ rcus   __ __ gar

      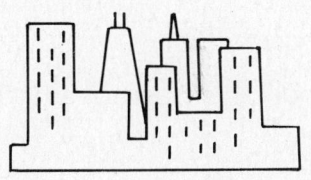

_____   _____   _____

Read the sentences. Fill in the correct letters to complete each word.

1. I _____n't find the thirty _____ts that I put in my wallet.
    ce   ca   cen   an

2. _____dy wants to buy four of those _____dy bars.
    Can Cin   cin   can

3. We c_____ a small room in a jail a c_____.
      ell   all   all   ell

4. There's a carton of milk in the _____ter of the _____ter for you.
                                    coun   cen   cen   coun

5. My _____cle is going to _____cle your birthdate with a red pen.
      un   cir   un   cir

6. The _____cus men put up two big _____vas tents.
       cir   can   cir   can

7. Alex and _____y are looking forward to going to the _____y together.
           Cath   Cit   cath   cit

8. It's a _____y that some _____y streets are so dirty.
         cit   pit   cit   pit

Soft c -ce- -ci-

In some words you find the **ce** or **ci** pattern in the middle of the word. Remember to—
1. Use the soft sound of c.
2. Say the vowel sound for e or i.

Look at the pictures. Read the sentence that tells about each picture.

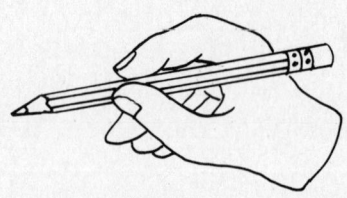

He will print with a **pencil.**

She is a **princess.**

Box in ce or ci in the words below. Read the words as you box in the letters.

ounces   dancer   stencil   concert   pencil

parcel   princess   pincers   fencer   percent

Choose the correct word from above for each picture. Write it neatly on the line.

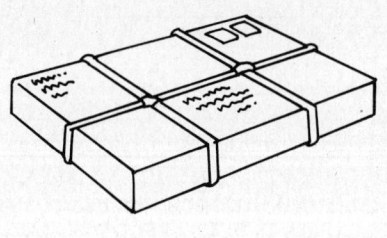

_____

_____

_____

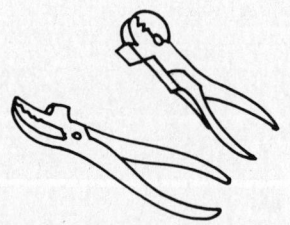

_____

_____

_____

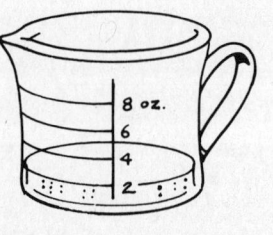

_____

_____

_____

Soft c -ce- -ci-

Read the words in each box. Divide the words into syllables or word parts that you can say. Circle the word that names the picture.

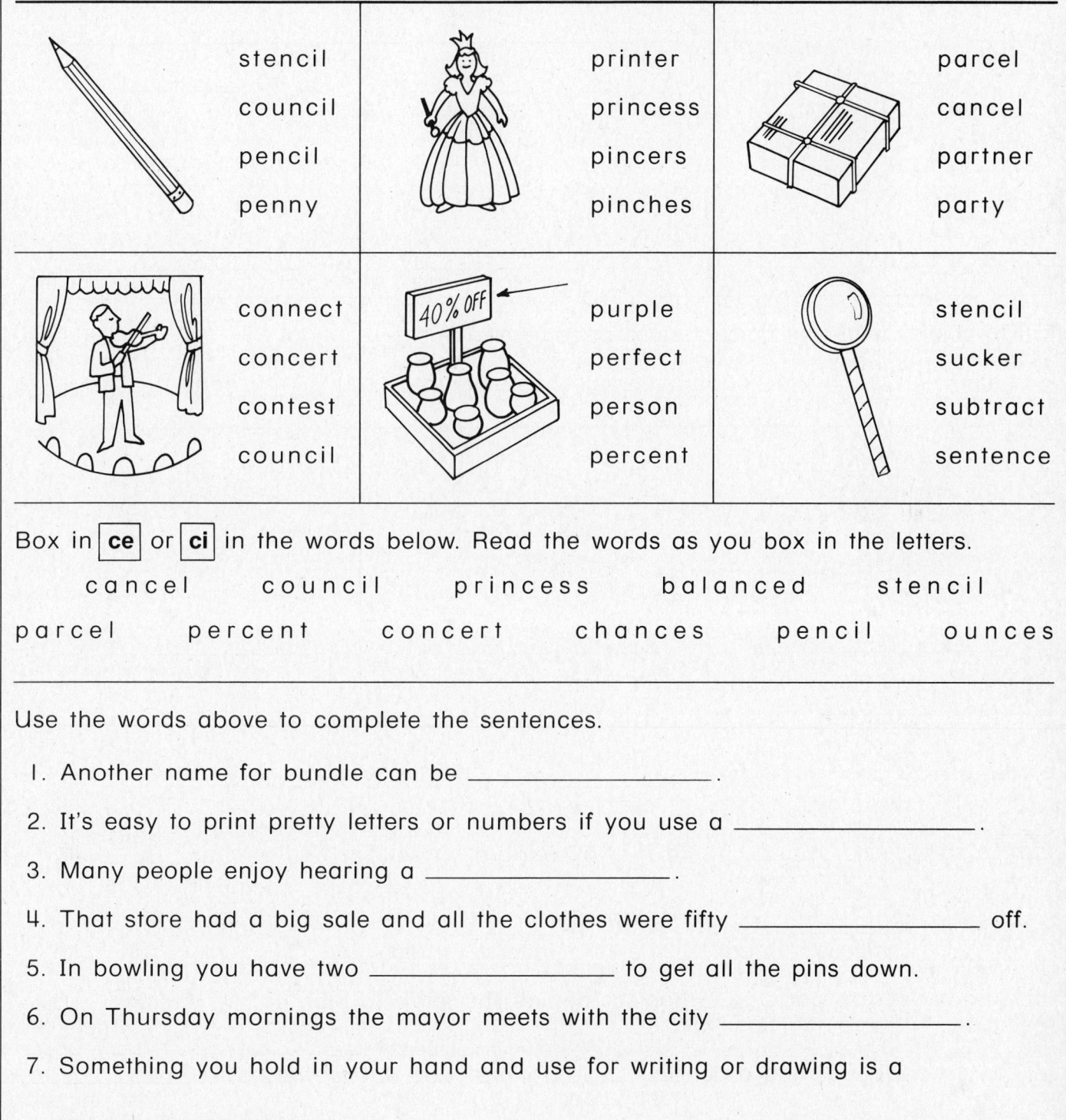

stencil	printer	parcel
council	princess	cancel
pencil	pincers	partner
penny	pinches	party
connect	purple	stencil
concert	perfect	sucker
contest	person	subtract
council	percent	sentence

Box in **ce** or **ci** in the words below. Read the words as you box in the letters.

cancel   council   princess   balanced   stencil

parcel   percent   concert   chances   pencil   ounces

Use the words above to complete the sentences.

1. Another name for bundle can be _____.

2. It's easy to print pretty letters or numbers if you use a _____.

3. Many people enjoy hearing a _____.

4. That store had a big sale and all the clothes were fifty _____ off.

5. In bowling you have two _____ to get all the pins down.

6. On Thursday mornings the mayor meets with the city _____.

7. Something you hold in your hand and use for writing or drawing is a

   _____.

8. The dancers in that show were _____ on their toes.

9. A girl who may become a queen when she grows up is called

   a _____.

10. Now I won't be going on the trip. I'll have to _____ my plans.

Soft c   -ce-   -ci-

Fill in **ce** in the words below. Write the correct word under the pictures.

Fran ___ ___ s   balan ___ ___ d   per ___ ___ nt   con ___ ___ rt

_____	_____	_____

Fill in **ci** and write the correct word under the pictures.

sten ___ ___ l   coun ___ ___ l   pen ___ ___ l   dan ___ ___ ng

_____	_____	_____

Read the sentences. Fill in the correct letters to complete each word.

1. The dan_____ named Dan_____ put on quite a good show.
          cer ny   cer ny

2. The sales per_____ said that gloves are on sale at fifty per_____ off.
          son cent   son cent

3. Frances pr_____ the word "pr_____" on the chalkboard.
       incess inted   incess inted

4. Mom needed to par_____ her car behind the store to pick up the big par_____.
          cel k   cel k

5. The school bands had a con_____ to see who put on the best con_____.
          test cert   test cert

6. I need to use that st_____ to make some st_____ on my picture.
         ars encil   ars encil

7. Our class had to can_____ the order for the can_____.
         dy cel   dy cel

8. Joe coun_____ thirty members in that picture of our city coun_____.
        cil ted   cil ted

Soft c

Here is a code.

1	**2**	**3**	**4**	**5**	**6**	**7**	**8**	**9**	**10**
ir	ur	oi	oy	ce	ci	a	e	ck	o

Write the correct letters neatly into the blanks in the words under the sentences. Then circle the word that completes each sentence.

When people are speaking to each other, we can hear both of their _____.

Vin___   v___ ___s   Vi___y   av___d   ___ ___rs
  5   3 5   9   3   8 7

Every grown-up person was _____ a child.

oun___   ___nk   on___   st___ry   on___
  5   3   5   10   8

Pencils and picket fences both have _____.

pl___nts   g___tes   prin___   poun___   p___nts
  7   7   5   5   3

Mr. Burke has gone to buy his family some tickets for the _____.

___rcle   c___nvas   ___rcus   c___ns   ___nts
  6   7   6   3   5

That express train goes a long _____ every day.

destr___   tran___   ___ty   tra___   distan___
  4   5   6   9   5

In English class yesterday, we put words together into _____.

entran___s   sin___   sp___ll   b___ ___k   senten___s
  5   5   8   10 10   5

Square, folk, and waltz are all different kinds of _____.

sh___pes   d___rk   dan___s   d___mp   poun___s
  7   7   5   7   5

An animal called a camel may have one hump in the _____ of his back.

___nt   c___m___l   ___nter   c___unt___r   ___ll___r
  5   7 8   5   10 8   5 7

The set of plastic nuts and bolts was his _____ for a birthday present.

choi___   ch___ ___s ___   ch___n___   c___n   ch___ck
  5   8 8 8   7 5   3   8

---

kn (silent k)

Some words have a letter that you do not sound out. A letter that you do not say is called a <u>silent</u> letter.

Look at the pictures. Read the sentences below the pictures. Fill in the blanks.

Kate tied a **knot** in the rope.

I do not say the ___ in <u>knot</u>.

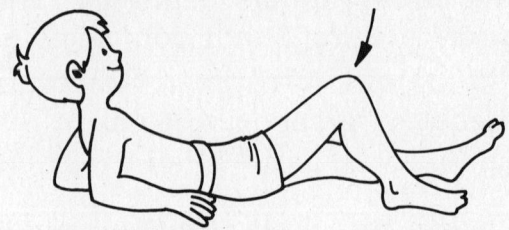

This is his **knee.**

I do not say the ___ in <u>knee</u>.

Cross out <u>silent k</u> in the words below. Read the words.

knife   knob   know   knot   knuckle

knives   knit   knead   kneel   knock

Choose the correct word from above for each picture. Write it neatly on the line.

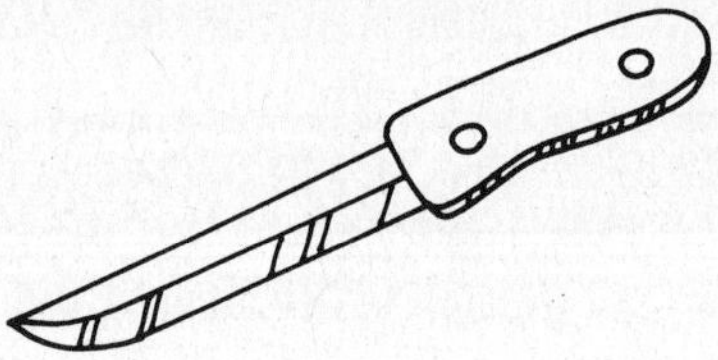

_____	_____	_____
_____	_____	_____
_____	_____	_____

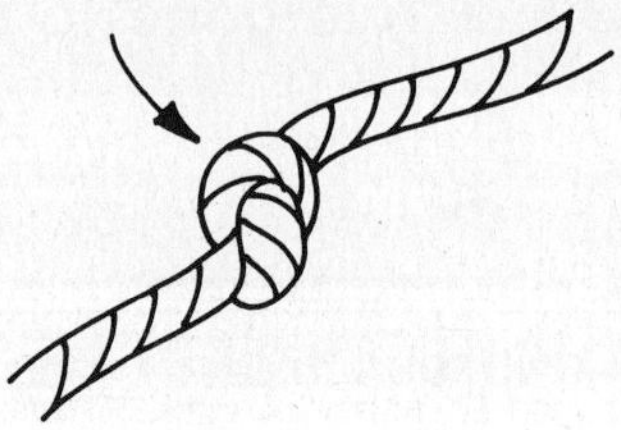

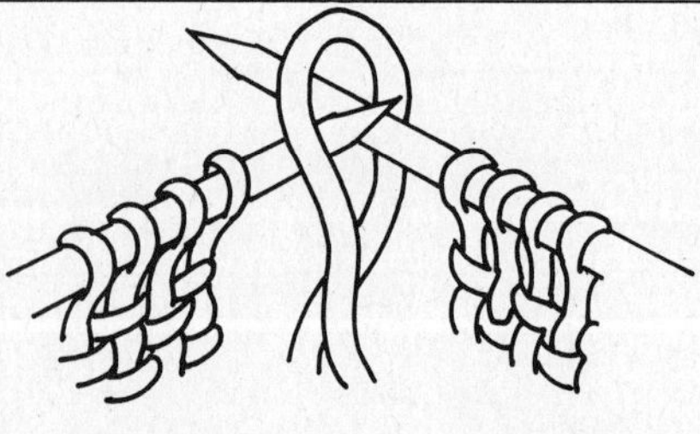

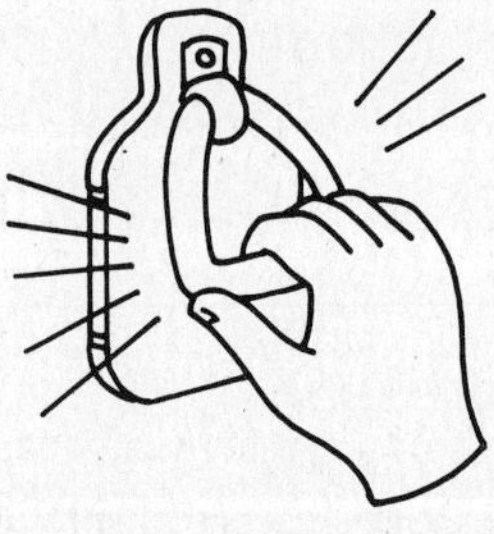

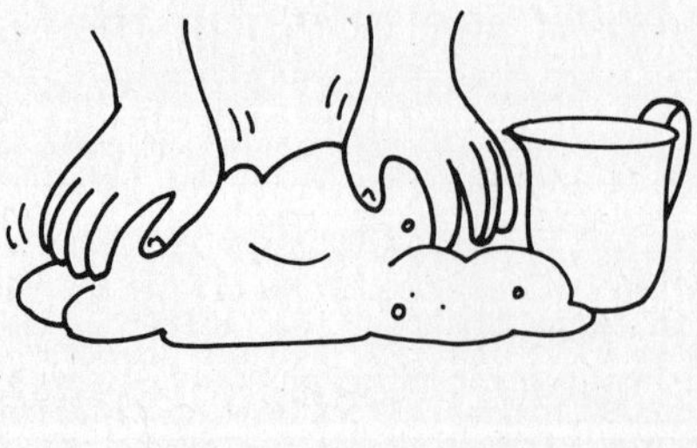

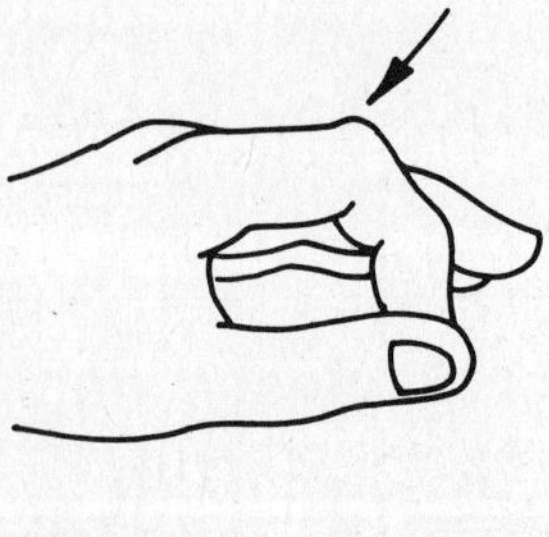

kn (silent <u>k</u>)

Read the words in each box. Then circle the correct word for each picture.

knee	knack	knot
keep	snack	know
keen	crack	knob
kneel	knock	knock

now	knife	kite
know	kite	kilt
snow	life	kept
known	knit	kneel

knob	own	kit
knot	known	knit
cot	crown	kind
knock	know	knife

Cross out <u>silent k</u> in the words below. Read the words.

knife   knob   know   knee

knot   knock   knit

Use the words above to fill in the blanks.

1. Another word for a round handle can be _____.

2. To understand something is to _____ it.

3. A rope or string can be tied into a _____.

4. The joint in your leg that bends when you stoop is your _____.

5. This may be used to cut something. _____

6. To loop yarn together with two long needles is to _____.

kn   (silent k)

Read the words in each box. Divide the longer words into syllables or word parts that you can say, if you need to. Circle the word that matches the picture.

keen		nickels		knapsack	
knee		knuckles		ketchup	
kneel		knickers		kicker	
keep		kicked		knick-knacks	

knickers		knuckles		knife	
knuckles		knickers		knives	
kernel		knapsack		kindle	
kitchen		knick-knacks		kind	

Cross out silent k in the words below. Read the words.

knife   kneeling   knocking   knees   knapsack   knots

knuckles   knickers   knives   known   kneel   knitted

Use the words above to complete these sentences.

1. A tool with a handle and a sharp blade used for cutting is a _____.

2. The joints in your fingers are called your _____.

3. A canvas bag worn on your back is called a _____.

4. The little girl fell down and hurt both of her _____.

5. Something that most of us know about is well _____.

6. When people eat, they use forks, spoons, and _____.

7. To bend down and rest on your knees is to _____.

8. When you tap with your knuckles, you are _____.

9. The scarf that Grandmother gave me was one she _____ herself.

10. Short baggy pants that are gathered at the knee are called _____.

kn   (silent <u>k</u>)

Fill in **kn** in the words below. Write the correct word neatly under each picture.

__ __ it   __ __ ives   __ __ eel   __ __ ife

__ __ ees   __ __ uckle   __ __ ock   __ __ ob

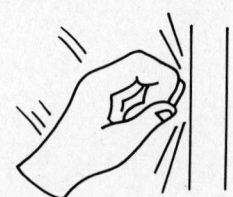

_____

_____

_____

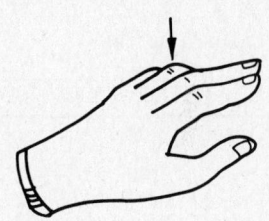

_____

_____

_____

Read the sentences. Fill in the correct letters to complete each word.

1. The hiker took off his _____ap and put it in his _____apsack.
   ⠀⠀⠀⠀⠀⠀⠀⠀⠀⠀⠀⠀⠀kn c⠀⠀⠀⠀⠀⠀⠀⠀⠀⠀⠀⠀⠀⠀⠀kn c

2. It is a well-_____own fact that kings and queens have _____owns.
   ⠀⠀⠀⠀⠀⠀⠀⠀⠀⠀cr kn⠀⠀⠀⠀⠀⠀⠀⠀⠀⠀⠀⠀⠀⠀⠀⠀⠀cr kn

3. The Boy Scouts sat on their _____ots and made _____ots the way their
   leader did.⠀⠀⠀⠀⠀⠀⠀⠀kn c⠀⠀⠀⠀⠀⠀⠀⠀⠀⠀⠀⠀kn c

4. My little sister _____ows what sound _____ows make.
   ⠀⠀⠀⠀⠀⠀⠀⠀kn c⠀⠀⠀⠀⠀⠀⠀⠀⠀⠀⠀⠀⠀kn c

5. Joyce must take care not to _____ock the _____ock off the shelf when
   she dusts.⠀⠀⠀⠀⠀⠀⠀⠀kn cl⠀⠀⠀⠀⠀⠀⠀⠀kn cl

6. My little brother scraped his _____uckle once on that big metal _____uckle.
   ⠀⠀⠀⠀⠀⠀⠀⠀⠀⠀⠀⠀⠀b kn⠀⠀⠀⠀⠀⠀⠀⠀⠀⠀⠀⠀⠀⠀⠀⠀⠀⠀⠀⠀⠀b kn

7. Frances took her plastic _____itting needles out of her _____it.
   ⠀⠀⠀⠀⠀⠀⠀⠀⠀⠀⠀⠀kn k⠀⠀⠀⠀⠀⠀⠀⠀⠀⠀⠀⠀⠀⠀⠀⠀kn k

8. Every farmer _____ows that a rooster _____ows just before sunrise.
   ⠀⠀⠀⠀⠀⠀⠀⠀cr kn⠀⠀⠀⠀⠀⠀⠀⠀⠀⠀⠀⠀⠀cr kn

kn (silent k)

Here are words that sound alike, but—

1. They have different spellings.
2. They have different meanings.

Say **knot.**

Which one is a <u>knot</u>?   Circle the <u>knot</u>.

Say **not.**

Which ones are <u>not</u> circles?   Circle them.

Fill in <u>not</u> or <u>knot</u>.

Boy Scouts need to know how to tie a good _____.

Kevin will _____ need a knapsack when he goes out.

Tie a good _____ in both of your ribbons so they won't get lost.

Say **knows.**

He <u>knows</u> how much 2 + 2 are.   2 + 2 are _____.

Say **nose.**

Why do you have a <u>nose</u>?   Your <u>nose</u> is used for _____.

seeing
hearing
smelling
tasting

Fill in <u>knows</u> or <u>nose</u>.

Now Burton _____ how to do his math problems.

Mr. Knox _____ how to knock down all the bowling pins at once.

Joyce has a cold, so her _____ is running.

Say **know.**

Do you <u>know</u> what month is after May?   Is it March or June? _____

Say **no.**

Are you a man?   Yes   No

Fill in <u>know</u> or <u>no</u>.

All the first-grade children now _____ their ABC's.

We _____ that in our family Uncle Robert has a knack for telling jokes.

Mrs. Burg said that she will buy _____ more knick-knacks for her house!

Soft c

In these words the <u>e</u> at the end tells you to do <u>two things</u>.
1. It tells you to say the <u>name</u> of the middle vowel, <u>not its sound</u>.
2. It tells you to use the <u>s</u> sound for the <u>c</u>.

Look at the pictures. Read the sentences that tell about the pictures.

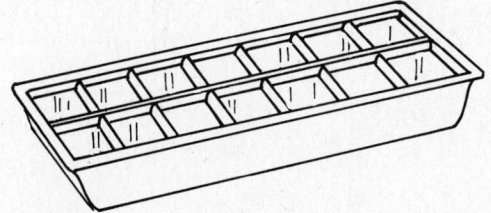

This is a tray of **ice** cubes.

This is a picture of a **face.**

Box in | ce | in these words. Read the words as you box in the letters.

m i c e	l a c e	B r u c e	a c e	s l i c e
r i c e	s p a c e	t r a c e	d i c e	p r i c e

Choose the correct word from above for each picture. Write it neatly on the line.

_____

_____

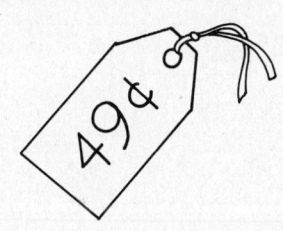

_____

_____

_____

_____

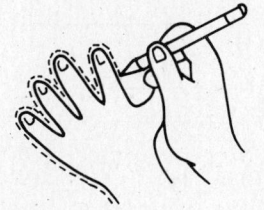

_____

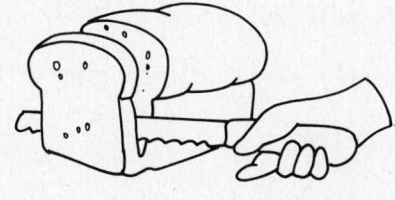

_____

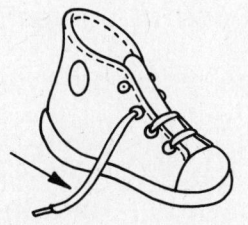

_____

Soft c

Read the words in each box. Circle the word that names the picture.

ace	race	branch
ice	rice	brace
use	rack	brake
act	rake	brass

lake	Dick	space
lace	disc	spice
lack	dose	slice
face	dice	slick

Box in ce in the words below. Read the words as you box in the letters.

price   dice   space   race   twice   trace

mice   ice   face   lace   ace   slice

Use the words above to complete these sentences.

1. The cost of something is its _____.

2. To do something two times is to do it _____.

3. A rocket is used to send spaceships into _____.

4. The way to cut meat or cheese is to _____ it.

5. Frozen water is _____.

6. A kind of contest to find out who or what is fastest is a _____.

7. The ruffle on a blouse or dress is sometimes made of _____.

8. Here is one mouse. There are two _____.

9. Your nose, mouth, and cheeks are all parts of your _____.

10. Small cubes with dots from one to six on their sides are _____.

Soft c

Read the words in each box. Circle the word that names the picture.

fireplug
fireproof
firewood
fireplace

iceboat
iceberg
Iceland
icebox

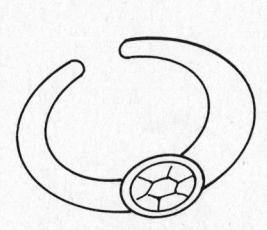

branches
braces
bracket
bracelet

racehorse
rackets
racetrack
raccoon

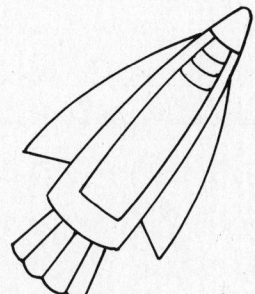

sparkplug
spacemen
spaceship
spending

birthplace
birthstone
birthday
birdhouse

Fill in the blanks with the words below.

| iceberg | braces | fireplace | nice | racehorse | rice | place |
| Grace | Iceland | bracelet | spices | spacecraft | traced | racetrack |

Bruce ate a bowl of _____.

He has _____ on his teeth.

Stand in one _____.

She _____ this picture.

Pepper and nutmeg are _____.

That was a _____ thing to do.

Her name is _____.

a _____ in orbit

a shiny gold _____

an _____ floating in the sea

a fast galloping _____

a smoky _____

cars on a _____

a visit to _____

Box in the base words. Then neatly circle the words that have soft c.

prices   licked   skater   spaces   racer

facts   laced   sliced   uses

faces   nicer   picked   traced   closes

Soft c

Fill in **ce** in the words below. Then write the correct word neatly under each picture.

la ___ ___   i ___ ___   mi ___ ___   sli ___ ___

tra ___ ___   ra ___ ___   fa ___ ___   pri ___ ___

_____   _____   _____

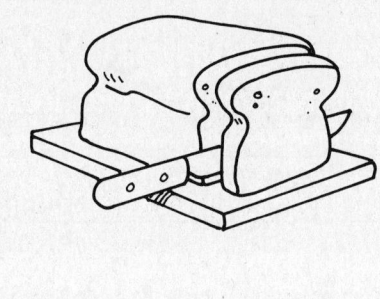

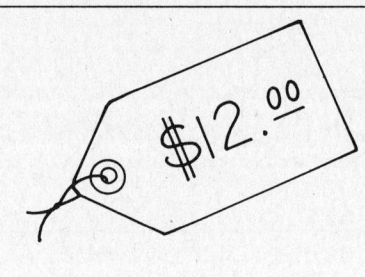

_____   _____   _____

Read the sentences. Fill in the correct letters to complete each word.

1. That big smile on her f_____ wasn't f_____.
                                 ace ake   ace ake

2. M_____ has gone to the pet shop to buy four white m_____.
    ice ike   ike ice

3. Don't pr_____ your finger on the pin in that pr_____ tag.
       ick ice   ick ice

4. I'll tr_____ this picture of a tr_____ for you.
      actor ace   actor ace

5. Br_____ is piling those br_____ by the truck.
    uce ucks   ice icks

6. We had to cancel the r_____ because it began to r_____.
      ain ace   ain ace

7. I wonder how that n_____ got in that n_____ bookcase.
      ice ick   ice ick

8. My brother R_____ likes salt and pepper on his r_____.
      ice ick   ice ick

Soft c variant endings

The words on this page end with a _vowel_ and _ce_, but you do not say the name of the vowel that comes before **ce**. Look at the pictures and words to see what happens.

| This is **ice.** | But this is **serv·ice.** | This is **lace.** | But this is a **neck·lace.** |

| This is a **face.** | But this is **sur·face.** | This is an **ace.** | But this is a **pal·ace.** |

Divide these words into two syllables. Write the syllables on the lines.

practice	_____ · _____	furnace	_____ · _____
office	_____ · _____	Alice	_____ · _____
justice	_____ · _____	lettuce	_____ · _____
necklace	_____ · _____	surface	_____ · _____

Use the words above to fill in the blanks.

1. It is used to heat houses in winter. _____

2. What must you do to become skilled at something? _____

3. It is green and leafy; we eat it in salad. _____

4. Where a doctor or dentist sees you is his or her _____.

5. You will enjoy this story called "_____ in Wonderland."

6. People on a jury will try hard for this. _____

7. The top layer of a paved road is the _____ of the road.

8. A string of beads worn around the neck is a _____.

Soft c

Read the words below. Then use them to complete the sentences.

palaces	announcer	advance	service	absence
balance	practice	police	distance	sentenced

1. Uncle Kevin lives just a short _____ from us.

2. Mrs. Knox said that both her boys have gone to football _____.

3. The squirrel kept its _____ as it ran across the clothesline to the porch roof.

4. We won't get very good seats if we don't buy our circus tickets

   in _____.

5. Places where kings or queens live may be called _____.

6. The _____ squad car raced after the maroon-colored van.

7. The waitress at that coffee shop was very polite and gave us very

   good _____.

8. The burglar was _____ to a long prison term for his crimes.

9. Curt was chosen to be the _____ for the school talent show.

entrance	office	furnaces	enforcing	lettuce
necklace	justice	surface	substance	convince

1. Last Saturday we visited Dr. Wallace in his _____ downtown.

2. In northern states, people need _____ to heat their homes.

3. The leaves floated slowly on the _____ of the water.

4. I don't think we can _____ Dad to let us stay out after dark.

5. We're going to meet Kathleen at the _____ to the circus.

6. One of the jobs of policemen and policewomen is _____ speed limits.

7. The woman was given a lovely _____ for her birthday.

8. Everyone in our family likes _____ on their ham and cheese sandwiches.

9. The jury hears all the facts in a case so that _____ will be done.

Soft c -cy

The words on this page end in **cy.** The **cy** pattern tells you to use the soft sound of c just as ce and ci do. The **cy** at the end of a word tells you to—
   1. Say the soft sound of c.
   2. Say the vowel sound ee for y at the end of a two-syllable word.

The little girl in this picture is **Nancy.**
Circle **Nancy.**

Cindy has a **fancy** dress. Nancy has a plain, simple dress. Circle Cindy.

In the words below, the vowel y is part of a vowel-consonant-vowel pattern.
It tells you to—
   1. Say the name of the middle vowel, not its sound.
   2. Say the soft sound of c.
   3. Say the vowel sound ee for y at the end of a two-syllable word.

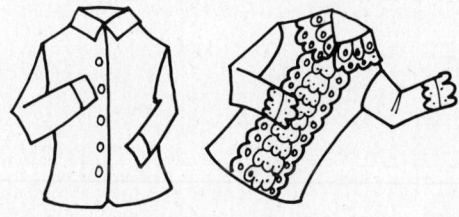

One of the blouses has a lot of lace.
Circle the **lacy** blouse.

One of these streets has ice on it.
Circle the **icy** street.

Spice was used on one of these foods.
Circle the one that is **spicy.**

The name of the tall girl is **Lucy.**
The short girl is **Tracy.** Circle **Lucy.**

Box in the vowel-consonant-vowel pattern in these words if there is one.

   l a c e   t r i c k y   i c y   l a c y   l u c k y   s p i c y   i c e

Write the base word.

   lacy _____   spicy _____   icy _____

Soft c   -cy

Put a mark on the line next to all the foods that taste spicy.

_____ some kinds of ketchup   _____ a garlic pickle

_____ an ice-cream cone   _____ a slice of birthday cake

_____ burnt toast   _____ some kinds of lunch meat

_____ radishes   _____ mustard

Mark when streets and sidewalks in the North can be icy.

_____ when they have oil on them   _____ after it rains and gets cold outside

_____ on a hot summer day   _____ in May or June

_____ in the month of March   _____ after a blizzard on a very cold day

---

Mark all the ones that tell about Nancy.

_____ goes out to buy dresses   _____ can be a girl

_____ can grow up to be a man   _____ can be a woman

_____ can become a nurse   _____ can have a brother

Mark all the ones that tell about Percy.

_____ can be a boy   _____ can have a brother or sister

_____ can grow up to be a man   _____ can be the first son in a family

_____ won't grow up to be a woman   _____ can be a grandmother

---

Mark all the things that can be fancy.

_____ a lacy, frilly blouse   _____ a dress that you buy for a party

_____ a plain gray shirt   _____ a pair of tennis shorts

_____ a wedding cake   _____ a hat with ribbons

Mark all the things that can be lacy.

_____ the tails of mice   _____ a wedding dress

_____ a gown for a princess   _____ a bowl full of rice

_____ a jacket for a policeman   _____ a pretty white blouse

Soft c   Hard c

Here are some words with soft c and some with c that sounds like k. The c that sounds like k is called **hard c**.

In the words below, box in hard c and the letter that follows it. Read all the words.

circle	crack	pencil	coin	city	can't
cling	cement	cents	council	cute	spicy
percent	Clancy	concern	office	voice	claps

Find the words with soft c. Write them on the lines.

spicy	_____	cigar	_____	lucky	_____
curdles		strict		fancy	
coil	_____	icy	_____	council	_____
incense		surface		lace	
concrete	_____	uncle	_____	back	_____
center		cabin		candy	

Find the syllables that will complete these words. Write them on the lines.

jus_____	sten_____	sur _____
cen_____	fan_____	fur_____
cir_____	cos_____	pen_____
prin_____	es_____	cac_____

-ter, -cus, -tice, -cess | -cy, -cil, -tume, -cape | -cil, -nace, -tus, -face

Don't forget what to do when you add endings to words that end in e!

Add -ed or -er

She is the announce_____.

He announce_____ the winner.

The store has a meat slice_____.

Dave slice_____ the cheddar cheese.

Jake lace_____ his ice skates.

Add -s or -er

Carlos likes to go to dance_____.

Miss Perez is a good dance_____.

He is a police office_____.

Their office_____ are downtown.

These spice_____ are very nice.

Soft c

Read the question. Read the choices. Put a neat X by the correct answer.

How are all of these things alike?

a ball that bounces
a circle
a crown for a prince or princess
a planet in outer space
the shape of a face

_____ They are made of rubber.
_____ They are made of gold.
_____ They are round.
_____ They are the names of shapes.

Where are all of these?

a place to buy tennis shoes
an office for the mayor
skyscrapers
streets with traffic
parking spaces for cars

_____ They are in the forest.
_____ They are in the city.
_____ They are on a farm.
_____ They are in stores.

How are these things alike?

ice-cream cones
rice
spicy hot dogs
a slice of mincemeat pie
eight ounces of milk

_____ They are all frozen.
_____ They are all things you cook in the oven.
_____ They are all white.
_____ They are all kinds of food.

How are these things alike?

going to the circus
going to a concert
dressing up like a princess
buying a fancy party dress
dancing to records

_____ They are sad things.
_____ They are places that you go to in a car.
_____ They are fun to do.
_____ They are places where you see clowns.

In what way are these two things alike?

a sentence
a story

_____ They both have words in them.
_____ They both can be printed on one line.

Which of these won't make a good birthday present for a girl or boy?

_____ a furnace   _____ a ball to bounce   _____ a fancy blouse   _____ a gold bracelet

_____ a price tag   _____ a bucket of ice   _____ a silver dollar   _____ a spruce tree

Which of these can you use to make posters?

_____ colored markers   _____ letter stencils   _____ a cup of rice

_____ some pencils   _____ an ounce of milk   _____ a ruler

Possessives

When you want to show that something belongs to someone, use **'s** after the name.

This purse <u>belongs to Joan</u>.
It is **Joan's** purse.

This bed is <u>for our dog</u>.
It is our **dog's** bed.

This mark $\boxed{'}$ is called an <u>apostrophe</u> (a·pos·tro·phe). It is the same mark that is used in writing contractions. To make this mark, start with a small circle above the line. Then hang a curved tail from it. Make some yourself. _____

In the blanks below each picture, write the word you need and **'s** after it. Do what the sentences tell you to do, or answer the questions.

The cowboy has a horse.

Circle the _____ horse.

Cindy has a pet bird. Is _____

pet bird an eagle? _____

The prince has a crown. Draw a star on

the _____ shiny gold crown.

This turtle has a green shell. Is this

_____ shell black? _____

Fill in the word you need in these sentences and put an **'s** after it.

1. Our family has a cat with long fur. It is our _____ cat.

2. Roy got a toy boat for his birthday. It was _____ birthday.

3. Arthur has a deep, loud voice. _____ voice is deep and loud.

4. Uncle Troy smokes cigars. We don't like the smell of Uncle _____ cigars.

5. Dad has a blue striped shirt. The blue striped shirt is _____ .

6. The woman is a nurse. A _____ job is to take care of sick people.

Possessives — Plurals

You know that when we want to say that there is <u>more than one</u> thing or person, we put an **s** on the end of the word.

Here is <u>one boy</u>.

Here are **two boys.**

To show that <u>something belongs to someone</u>, we put **'s** at the end of the word.

The dog <u>belongs to Fred</u>.
It is **Fred's** dog.

The skates <u>belong to Jane</u>.
They are **Jane's** skates.

Add **s** to the underlined words below to mean <u>more than one</u>.
Circle the word in the sentence that tells you there is <u>more than one thing</u>.
Add **'s** to show that <u>something belongs to a person or thing</u>.

1. I know those (two) <u>girl</u>s won't hurt the little kitten.

2. Don't let the dog play with the little <u>girl</u> stuffed animals.

3. I wonder if some <u>robin</u> will make their nests in our birdhouses.

4. Dad told us not to disturb the <u>robin</u> nest.

5. The <u>candle</u> flame flickered before it went out.

6. There are eight yellow <u>candle</u> on that fancy birthday cake.

7. Alice wants to buy both <u>book</u> about wild animals.

8. He has gone to get tape to fix this <u>book</u> torn pages.

9. The pencil sharpener is behind the <u>teacher</u> desk.

10. Most <u>teacher</u> don't like it when their classes get too noisy.

11. We'll go in their car because our <u>car</u> turn signal is broken.

12. Safety belts are put in all <u>car</u> that are being made today.

Review 2

Use the words below to fill in the blanks under the pictures.

fireplace	watercolors	iceberg	spacecraft
surfboard	clothespins	kneecap	hummingbird
sunburn	turtleneck	oilcan	pocketknife
cowboy	dragonfly	birthday	watermelon

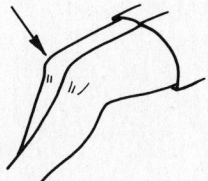

_____

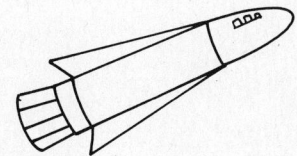

_____

_____

_____

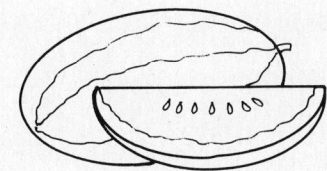

_____

_____

_____

_____

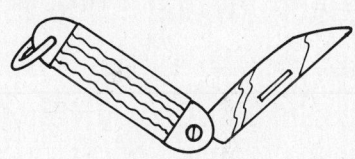

_____

_____

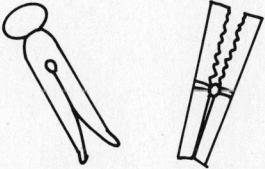

_____

_____

_____

_____

_____

Review 2

Read each question. Choose one answer. Mark your answer with an X.
Hint: The first word in each question will give you a clue to the answer.

Why did Mr. Turner buy both those model cars?

_____ at a toy store in the city

_____ at the closest shopping center

_____ because he won't need both of them

_____ because his two sons each wanted one

_____ because that one is the finest

What don't you need when you go exploring?

_____ two concert tickets

_____ a compass and map

_____ sturdy hiking boots

_____ a knapsack with food

_____ a first-aid kit

When do you want to make Dad's present?

_____ in a place where Dad won't see us

_____ in about thirty minutes (min·its)

_____ in the upstairs bedroom

_____ a nice pen and pencil set

_____ in the basement workshop

Who helps people when they're hurt?

_____ a princess

_____ some ointment

_____ some pills

_____ a doctor

_____ the nurse's office

Why did the little boy cry?

_____ when he hurt his knuckles

_____ because he scraped his knee

_____ after he fell on the icy walk

_____ because his pain was gone

_____ on the playground

Whose pet goes the fastest?

_____ Lorraine's big worm

_____ our family's cat

_____ their white horse

_____ my uncle's goldfish

_____ a snapping turtle

Where did you buy both of those toys?

_____ at the toy store on Central Street

_____ their children both wanted one

_____ last Saturday afternoon

_____ they wanted to have two of them

_____ next Thursday morning

Where can people enjoy ice skating?

_____ on ice cubes

_____ in the summer

_____ in a blizzard

_____ on frozen skating rinks

_____ gliding on ice is fun

Review 2

Read the sentences. Circle the word that completes each sentence.

What's being done about the boy's bike that was (stubborn, stolen)?

Let's get out of the sun and sit under that (shady, sunny) oak tree.

That story began with, "Once there was a (scaly, stony) fire-breathing dragon."

Here's the lettuce you wanted to put in your (sailor, salad).

They've gone to Taylor's Apple Orchard because the finest (apples, places) are grown there.

Our family goes to the circus whenever it comes to our (icy, city).

Our coach explained the rules once and asked if we had any (quizzes, questions).

We put up a fence so we won't need to worry about our dog (running, riding) away.

If Bruce keeps pulling the cat's tail, he may get (scratched, scrambled).

Mom takes the expressway to get to the (often, office) downtown where she works.

The directions said to circle the correct answer to (both, bolt) those questions.

Where's the closest (palace, place) to buy a nice birthday card?

Here's a policeman who can give us directions to the (points, post) office.

We're going to meet the others at the (entrance, enters) to the children's zoo.

I'm practicing my dance for the school (tallest, talent) show next Thursday.

Dad gave me a choice between animal crackers and popcorn for a (snatch, snack).

I'm convinced that Joan's stuffed turtle is the cutest one (I'm, I've) ever seen.

Trading your knapsack for an ice-cream bar was not the (wisest, wishes) thing to do.

The mayor sent out salt trucks so the icy city streets won't be a (hazard, blizzard).

I don't know who's working in the school (lunchbox, lunchroom) on Tuesday.

Mrs. Quincy asked us whose turn it is to play with the toy (raining, racing) cars.

Everyone in our family, except my little sister, likes (shiny, spicy) food.

Soft g   -ge

In the words below you see the **ge** pattern. It tells you to use the j̲ sound for g̲.
The g̲ that sounds like j̲ is called **soft g**.

Look at the pictures. Read the sentences that tell about the pictures.

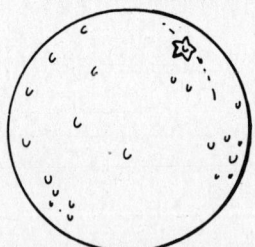

An **orange** is good to eat.

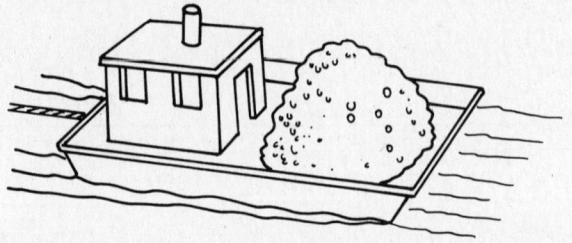

This kind of boat is called a **barge.**

Box in ge in the words below. Read the words as you box in the letters.

hinge   charge   urge   fringe   Marge

lounge   bulge   large   sponge   barge

Choose the correct word from above for each picture. Write it neatly on the line.

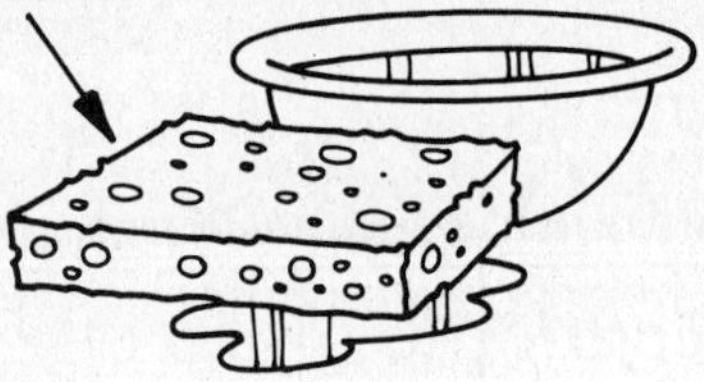

_____	_____	_____
_____	_____	_____
_____	_____	_____

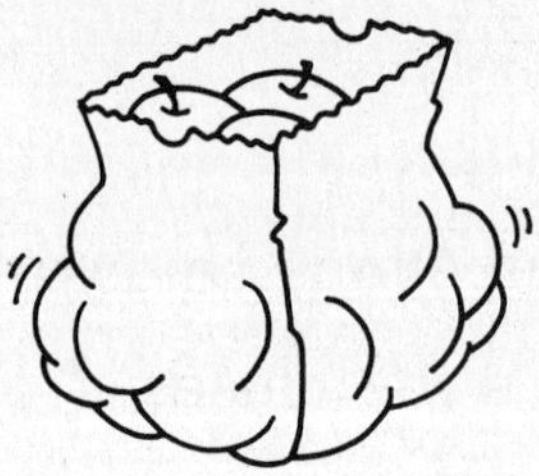

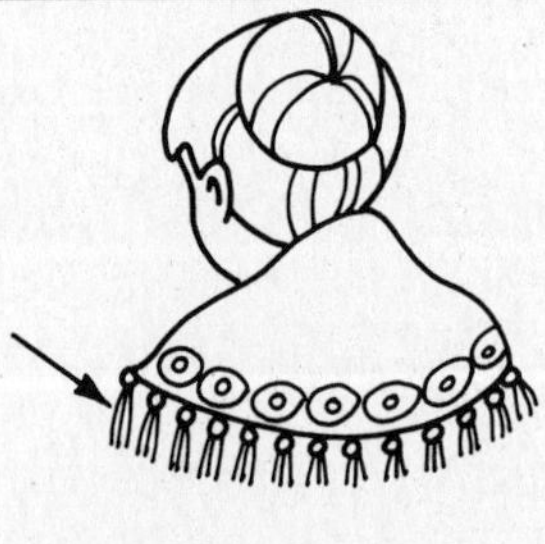

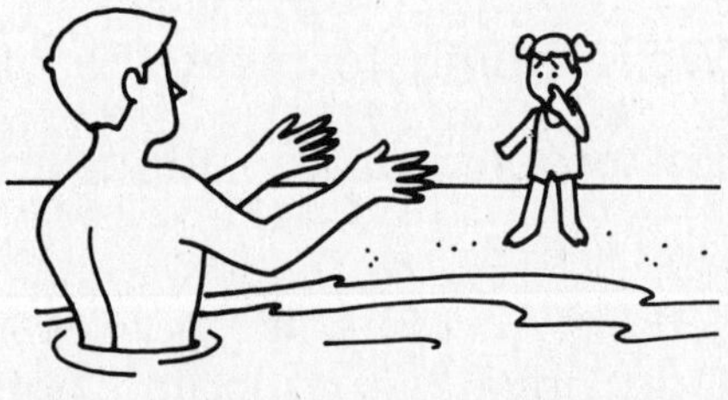

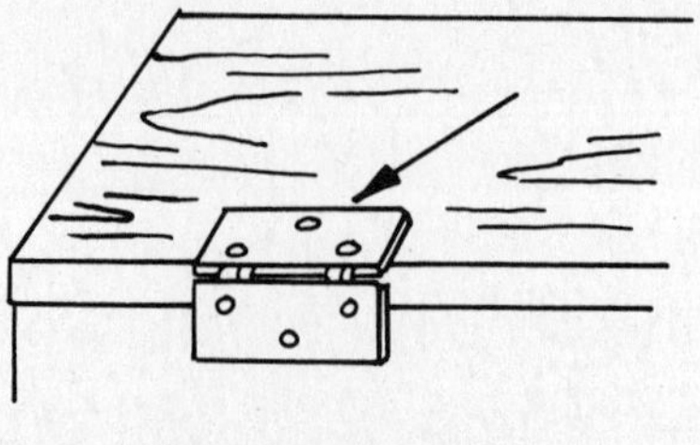

Soft g   -ge

Read the words in each box. Then circle the word that names the picture.

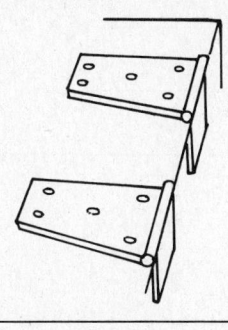

hitches
hangs
hinges
humps

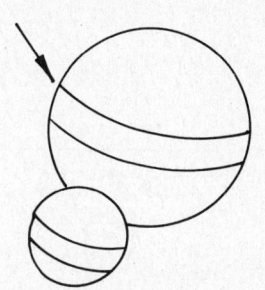

lounge
large
lance
barge

urns
urges
ushers
uses

spoons
sprang
spanks
sponges

lounges
lunches
lungs
louder

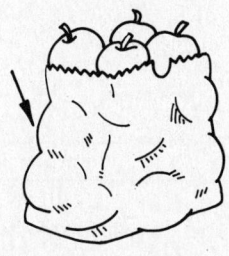

bulbs
barges
bulges
bangs

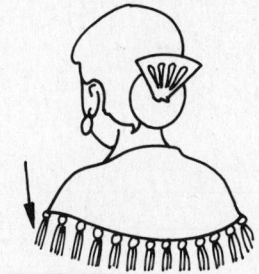

fangs
finish
French
fringe

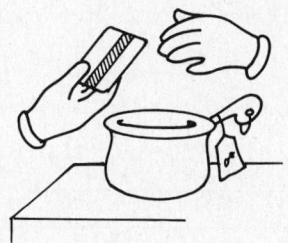

chances
charges
barges
charts

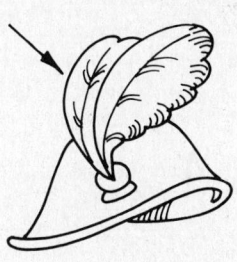

plugs
plums
plunges
plumes

Box in **ge** in the words below. Read the words as you box in the letters.

urge   hinges   plunge   barge

fringe   lounges   charge

Use the words above to fill in the blanks.

1. These allow a gate to swing back and forth. _____

2. Short strings used as trimming on a jacket or scarf are called _____ .

3. A large flat-bottomed boat that has no power and must be towed

   is a _____ .

4. To try hard to convince or coax someone is to _____ him or her.

5. Another word for the cost, fee, or price of a service is _____ .

6. Couches without armrests used by people to lie on and rest are _____ .

Soft g   -ge

Fill in **ge** in the words below. Then write the correct word neatly under each picture.

hin __ __   spon __ __   frin __ __   bar __ __

lar __ __   char __ __   plun __ __   ur __ __

_____

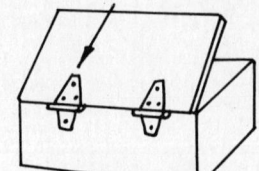

_____

_____

_____

_____

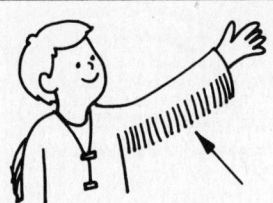

_____

Read the sentences. Fill in the correct letters to complete each word.

1. Quick! Wipe that sp_____ off the carpet with a wet soapy sp_____.
                  ot   onge   ot   onge

2. Vince will need four brass h_____ when he h_____ up the shutters.
                                inges angs   inges angs

3. His backpack b_____ with all the b_____ things he took to camp.
                  ulky   ulged   ulky   ulged

4. She looked at her price char_____ to see what to char_____ for the oranges.
                               ge   t   ge   t

5. He ur_____ us to go to see the big bronze ur_____ from Japan.
        ged   ns   ged   ns

6. The tugboat towed a b_____ down the river to a town called Hamb_____.
                 urg   arge   urg   arge

7. Our cat l_____ in the small room where there are no l_____ noises.
             oud   ounges   oud   ounges

Soft g   -dge

In the words on this page you see the **dge** pattern. You read it just like the **ge** pattern. Remember the sound you use when you see **ge** and do the same for **dge**. The letter <u>d</u> is silent in these words.

Look at the pictures. Read the sentences that tell about the pictures.

The **judge** has on a black robe.

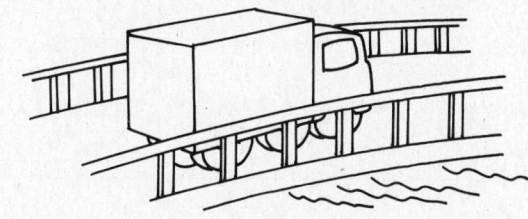

The truck is driving on the **bridge.**

Box in **dge** in these words. Read the words as you box in the letters.

b a d g e	e d g e	f u d g e	s m u d g e	w e d g e
p l e d g e	l e d g e	d o d g e	j u d g e	h e d g e

Choose the correct word from above for each picture. Write it neatly on the line.

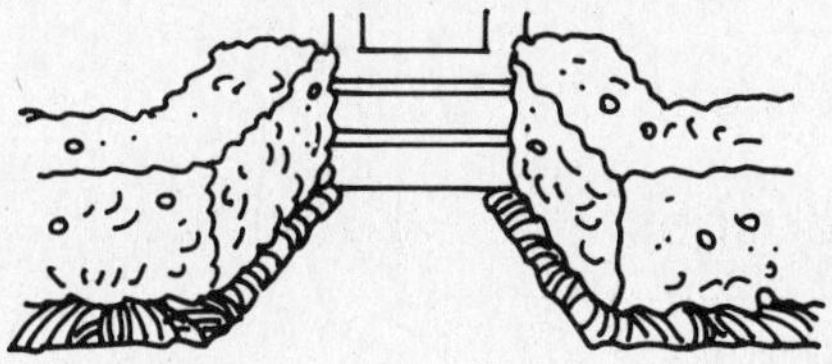

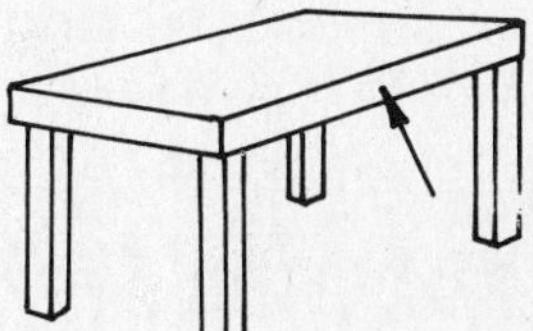

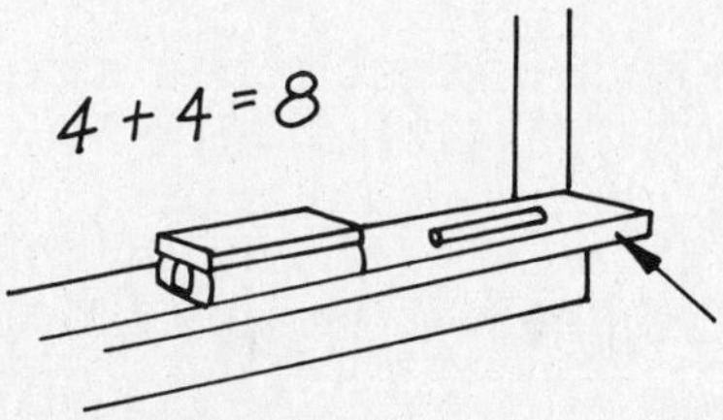

Soft g   -dge

Read the words in each box. Circle the word that matches the picture.

ridges wishes wedges witches	brush bring bridge bricks	trudge drudge trash trust
hedge hides hutch hitch	batches badges backs bands	ends edges eggs itches
badges batches dashes dutch	fetch fund fudge fish	lodge lash ledge large

Box in **dge** in the words below. Read the words as you box in the letters.

edge   badge   bridge   fudge

judges   ridge   hedge

Use the words above to fill in the blanks.

1. A kind of candy that tastes very sweet is _____ .

2. Something that's pinned or stitched to a shirt or jacket. _____

3. This connects two sides of a river so people and cars can cross it.

_____

4. Bushes or shrubs planted close together in a row form a _____ .

5. The sharp part of a cutting tool is the _____ of the blade.

6. The persons who choose the winner in a contest are the _____ .

Soft g -dge

Fill in **dge** in the words below. Then write the correct word neatly under each picture.

smu __ __ __   e __ __ __   do __ __ __   bri __ __ __

lo __ __ __   he __ __ __   nu __ __ __   we __ __ __

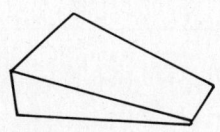

_____

_____

_____

_____

_____

_____

Read the sentences. Fill in the correct letters to complete the words.

1. Around the l_____ were small cabins made of l_____ for people to stay in.
               odge   ogs   odge   ogs

2. All that f_____ I ate is making me feel very f_____.
          ull   udge   ull   udge

3. The trucks will br_____ the large logs across that br_____.
          idge   ing   idge   ing

4. The j_____ has a glass and a large j_____ of water on his desk.
       ug   udge   ug   udge

5. The paint sm_____ in the art room all have sm_____ on them.
         udges   ocks   udges   ocks

6. When Jeff plays hide and seek, he often h_____ behind the h_____.
         ides   edges   ides   edges

7. The teacher asked us to pl_____ stand and say the pl_____.
         ease   edge   ease   edge

8. My d_____ goes after the ball when we play d_____ ball.
       odge   og   odge   og

Soft g

Which word belongs in each sentence? Write it on the line.

After Joyce finishes dinner, she'll have a _____ slice of lemon pie.

We enjoyed traveling to the _____ and hiking in the woods.

Put that flower pot in the center of the _____ so it won't fall.

lodge
ledge
large
long

How much did they charge to fix that broken _____ on the car?

They're playing policemen and making _____ out of cardboard and foil.

Sometimes our puppy won't _____ from the center of my bed.

badges
bandit
budge
bumper

The pretty woman in the fancy wedding gown is the _____.

Do you think that the _____ in Dad's pocket is a surprise for us?

People enjoy walking on that nice sidewalk along the _____.

bridge
bulge
bring
bride

Both of their cats know there's a nest of robins in the _____.

The dog in that house kept _____ because his family was gone.

Once a month Mr. Royce goes to the _____ on Central Street.

barge
barking
barn
barber

When Mom finished knitting Nancy's scarf, she put _____ along the edge.

Cindy had a chance to take a large bite of Marge's _____.

It was so _____, she nearly hit the animal with her car.

foggy
fudge
forge
fringe

Who's going to _____ off the counter after we finish dinner?

Vince's shirt needs cleaning because it has dirty _____ on it.

Many people on our block are buying seeds for _____ planting.

sponge
spring
smudges
sledge

When Frances goes shopping on Thursday, she'll buy eight

ripe _____.

Grace's _____ has gone to buy the shiny red wagon she wants.

I'm using my teacher's stencil to draw four furry _____.

dodge
dogs
oranges
dad

Soft g   ge-   gi-

Here are some words that begin with **ge** and some that begin with **gi**. The rule for **gi** is the same as for **ge**: Use the soft sound of g. When you see **ge** or **gi** at the beginning of a word—
1. Use the soft sound of g.
2. Say the vowel sound for e or i, or the sound for the er or ir pattern.

This kind of stone is a **gem**.

A **giraffe** is a very tall animal.

Box in ge or gi in the words below. Then write them below the correct pictures.

gerbil   gentle   German   gems   germs   ginger   gel

_____

_____

_____ shepherd

_____ ale

_____

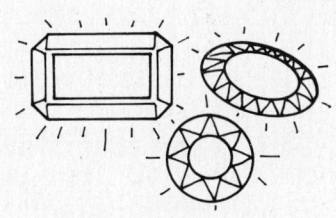

_____

Find the words that do not have soft g. Draw a circle around them. Read the words.

| gerbil | gum | gone | bags | bulge |
| gargle | ginger | gem | gold | gentle |

Connect the syllables to make complete words.

ger	den	gir	ger
gar	bil	gur	affe
gal	lop	gin	gle

© 1995 SRA/McGraw-Hill

Soft g ge- gi-

Read the words in each box. Divide the longer words into syllables or word parts that you can say. Keep the letters **ge** and **gi** together. Circle the word that names the picture.

grim	grabbing	gladly
germs	ground	gallop
German	grumble	gentle
gems	giraffe	center

pen	glimmer	glider
gem	grinned	griddle
gum	grinder	gerbil
yam	ginger ale	glitter

Box in gi or ge in each word below. Read the words as you box in the letters.

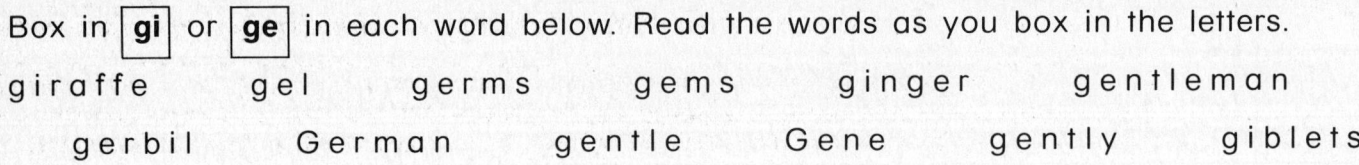

giraffe   gel   germs   gems   ginger   gentleman

gerbil   German   gentle   Gene   gently   giblets

Use the words above to fill in the blanks.

1. This is the tallest living animal. _____

2. They are too small to see, but they can make you sick. _____

3. This breed of dog helps police and blind people. _____ shepherd

4. A man who has very good manners may be called a _____.

5. The spicy root of this plant is used for making a sweet drink. _____

6. This small, furry animal makes a nice pet. _____

7. The finest stones used in rings, bracelets, and necklaces are _____.

8. When animals are tame and do not attack people, we say they are

   _____.

9. This can be a boy's first name. _____

10. Bruce knows that he has to handle his puppy very _____.

Soft g ge- gi-

Fill in **Ge** in the words below. Write the correct word under each picture.

___ ___ rms   ___ ___ rbil   ___ ___ rman   ___ ___ ntle

_____	_____	_____

Fill in **Gi** and write the words under the correct pictures.

___ ___ nger   ___ ___ nny   ___ ___ raffe   ___ ___ blets

_____	_____ ale	_____

Read the sentences. Fill in the correct word in each blank.

Ginger   urged   gobble

Marge _____ us to name our pet hamster _____ .

garden   grater   German

Mom was angry when our _____ shepherd dug up the _____ .

giraffe   gentle   grass

A spotted _____ stood in the tall _____ nibbling leaves from a tree.

Ginny   germs   green

_____ will take back the nice _____ skirt because it's too small.

gather   Glen   gentle

The nurse was very _____ when she gave _____ his shot.

Soft g

Read each sentence. Write the correct word in the blanks.

They both wanted another _____ because they were very hungry.
edge   egg

What kind of animal did you see scurry under that pile of _____?
logs   lodges

All of the people in my family enjoy drinking _____ ale.
grinder   ginger

Will whoever goes to the _____ store please buy me a comic book?
drudge   drug

How many times has Vincent's family gone to that fishing _____?
lodge   logs

All of the boys and girls joined hands to _____ the songs.
singe   sing

Our class says the _____ to the flag every morning.
pledge   plugs

The _____ asked the jury for its verdict in the case of the burglar.
judge   jugs

Dad needs to use that _____ knife to slice the roast beef.
lamp   large

I know that Marge's toy chest has big shiny brass _____.
hinges   hangs

The woolen scarves in that women's store have _____ on them.
figs   fringe

I cover my nose when I sneeze so that I don't pass my _____ along.
germs   grins

The street sweeper goes along the curb and _____ up all the dirt.
gentle   gathers

Before I buy that record player, I want to _____ it in to try it first.
plunge   plug

Madge wants to know how much the store _____ for a box of pencils.
charges   chugs

Kirk used the _____-shaped block to make a ramp for his toy cars.
webs   wedge

Mr. Price is downstairs at _____ house fixing their furnace.
Gene's   gains

Soft g

The letter e at the end of the words on this page tells you to do two things.
 1. It tells you to say the name of the middle vowel, not its sound.
 2. It tells you to use the soft sound of g.

Look at the pictures. Read the sentence that tells about each picture.

I will read this **page.**

This is a **huge** animal.

Box in | ge | in the words below. Read the words as you box in the letters.

stage cage change huge

age rage page

Write the correct word under each picture.

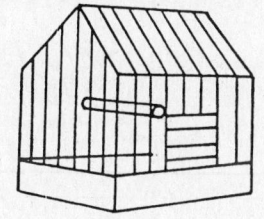

_____

_____

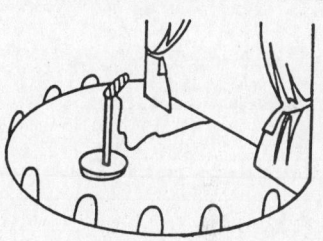

_____

_____

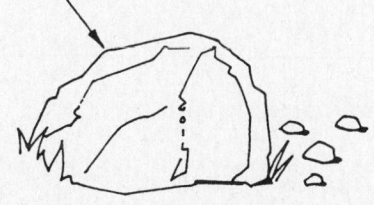

_____

_____

Box in | ge | if you see it in these words. Read all the words.

rags rage hugs pangs huge

chance hangs page change stage

Soft g

Read the words in each box. Circle the word that names the picture.

cast cash cape cage	rage race rack rare	charge chance change champ
hugs huge use hung	ranch ramps range rang	strange gates stay stage
rage rags rays rash	straggle stage strange strong	age ace ape ago

Box in **ge** in the words below. Read the words as you box in the letters.

huge   strange   cage   age

range   wage   rage

Use the words above to complete the sentences.

1. You can say that something that is odd or different is _____.

2. The number of years you have lived is your _____.

3. Something that is very, very large is _____.

4. The amount someone pays you for the work you do is your _____.

5. If someone becomes very angry and has a temper tantrum, we say he's in

   a _____.

6. Another name for a kitchen stove is _____.

Soft g

Fill in **ge** in the words below. Write the correct word on the line under each picture.

sta ___ ___   a ___ ___   hu ___ ___   ran ___ ___   ra ___ ___

_____   _____   _____   _____

Read the sentences. Fill in the correct word in each blank.

huge   hung   hug

Grandmother gave little Jane a _____ _____.

pigs   pages   pangs

On the next _____ are pictures of the cutest _____ I've ever seen.

eggs   ages   apes

I asked the man who was feeding the _____ at the zoo what their _____ were.

cage   came   cape

The bird that we got from the pet store _____ with its own _____.

stag   tag   stage

The price _____ was still on the puppet _____ Dad gave me.

wags   wages   white

Whenever that little _____ puppy sees people he loves, he _____ his tail.

wages   wags   weeks

He is paid his _____ once every two _____.

raked   rage   rang

Two boys _____ our bell and asked if we wanted our leaves _____.

wr (silent w)

In words that begin with **wr** you do not say the **w**. The w is silent.

Look at the pictures. Read the sentences below the pictures. Fill in the blanks.

 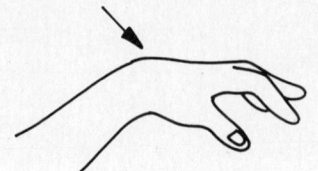

Marge knows how to **write** her name.

I do not say the ___ in write.

This is her **wrist.**

I do not say the ___ in wrist.

Cross out silent w in the words below. Read the words.

wren   wrench   write   wing   wrist

wring   wrap   wreath   wrong   wreck

Choose the correct word from above for each picture. Write it neatly on the line.

  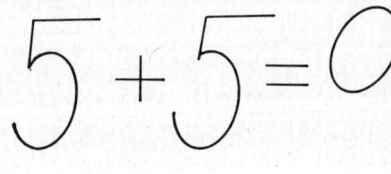

_____   _____   _____

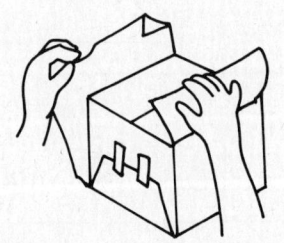  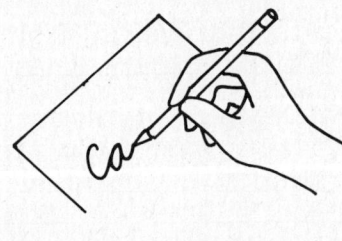

_____   _____   _____

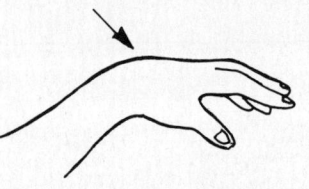 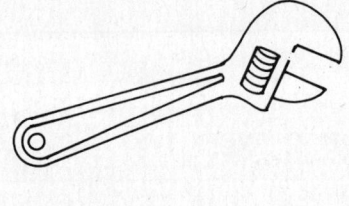 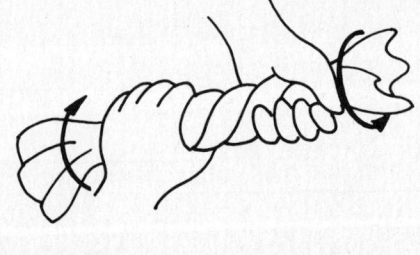

_____   _____   _____

wr (silent w)

Read the words in each box. Then circle the word that matches the picture.

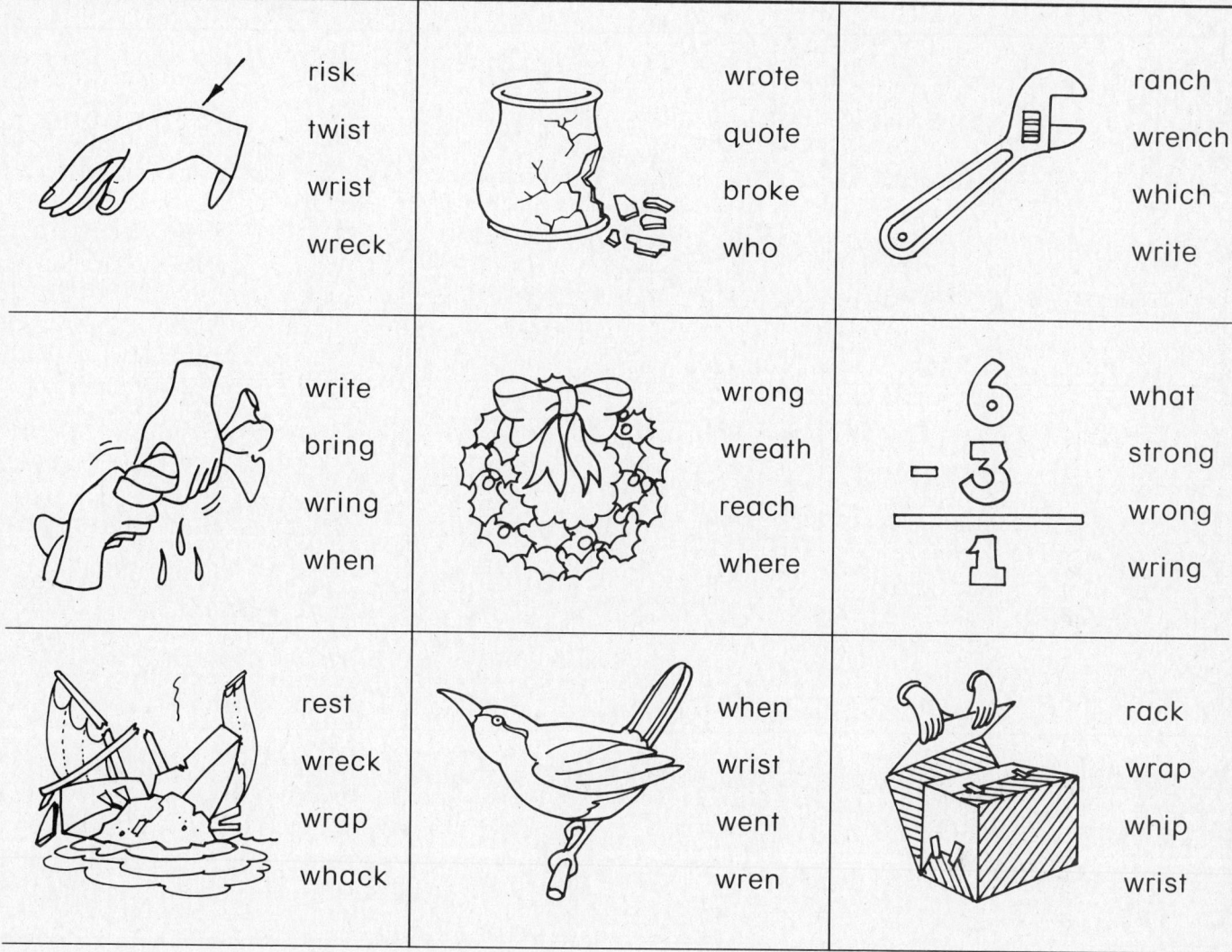

risk twist wrist wreck	wrote quote broke who	ranch wrench which write
write bring wring when	wrong wreath reach where	what strong wrong wring
rest wreck wrap whack	when wrist went wren	rack wrap whip wrist

Cross out silent w in the words below. Read the words.

wrench   wrong   wrap   write

wreath   wrist   wreck

Use the words above to complete the sentences.

1. A tool used for holding and turning nuts and bolts is a _____.

2. A ring of leaves or flowers is a _____.

3. To fold a covering around something is to _____ it.

4. The joint where your hand and arm join together is your _____.

5. To form letters and words with a pen or pencil is to _____.

6. The opposite of correct is _____.

wr (silent w)

Read the words in each box. Divide the words into syllables or word parts that you can say. Keep the letter pair **wr** together. Circle the word that names the picture.

shipwreck
subtract
squirrel
shimmer

whiter
water
writer
waiter

wilting
writing
waiting
wringing

wrapping
wringing
writing
wrecking

whopper
wrecker
whisper
wrapper

written
whispers
wrinkles
waitress

Cross out silent w in the words below. Read the words.

wreath   writer   writing   wrist   wrote   wrenches

wrapper   shipwreck   wren   wrinkle   wrong   wring

Use the words above to complete these sentences.

1. A small bird with a long bill and stubby tail is a _____.

2. All of the sailors escaped from the _____ in lifeboats.

3. A watch that's worn on your _____ is called a _____watch.

4. If you don't hang up your clothes, they'll _____.

5. The covering around something like gum or candy bars is the _____.

6. A person who writes books is often called a _____.

7. In school we practice _____ words every day.

8. _____ means the same as not correct.

9. To twist something in order to squeeze the water out is to _____ it.

10. Nancy dropped the letter she _____ into the mailbox.

wr (silent w)

Choose the correct word for each sentence. Write it neatly on the line.

My family has a pretty _____ of dry flowers in our kitchen.	wrens
Gene's father enjoyed making those birdhouses for the _____.	wreath
Something badly broken or destroyed can be called a _____.	wrist
	wreck

Mom won't buy that skirt for me because it's the _____ size.	wrung
Sue has gone upstairs to get both gifts that need to be _____.	wrapped
I get annoyed when people throw candy _____ on the ground.	wrappers
	wrong

That nice gentleman is a _____ of children's books.	write
On Friday, I _____ a two-page letter to my uncle in Iceland.	writer
That postcard had a strange note _____ on the back of it.	written
	wrote

A policeman called a tow truck to take away the _____ car.	wrinkles
Carlos _____ up his messy worksheet and tossed it in a wastebasket.	wristwatch
The judge's gray hair and _____ told us he was quite old.	wrecked
	wrinkled

Florence didn't know the time because her _____ had stopped.	wrinkled
The children in her class know how to _____ their names.	wrist
Marcy lost her gold bracelet when it fell off her _____.	wristwatch
	write

I _____ out the washcloth and hung it on the towel bar to dry.	wrong
Dad has gone out to buy a _____ so he can fix the leaky pipe.	wring
Clothing will dry faster if you _____ it out before you hang it up.	wrung
	wrench

I'm _____ the fudge in foil so it won't become stale.	writing
At two o'clock the class will practice their hand-_____ skills.	wrecking
Put those animals outside because they're _____ the house.	wringing
	wrapping

118

Soft g   -ge-   -gi-

Here are some two-syllable words with **ge** or **gi** in the middle of the word.
Remember, when e or i comes just after the g in the middle of a word—
   1. Use the soft sound of g.
   2. Say the vowel sound for e or i, or the sound you know for the **er** pattern.

Look at the pictures. Read the sentence that tells about each picture.

He is doing a **magic** trick.

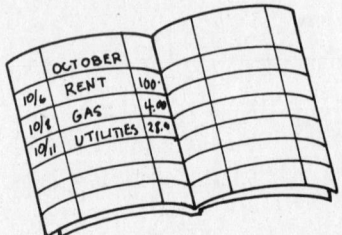

A **ledger** is for keeping records.

Box in ge or gi in these words. Read the words as you box in the letters.

magic   margin   ledger   danger   badger

Bridget   stranger   plunger   ranger   fidget

Choose the correct word from above for each picture. Write it neatly on the line.

_____   _____   _____

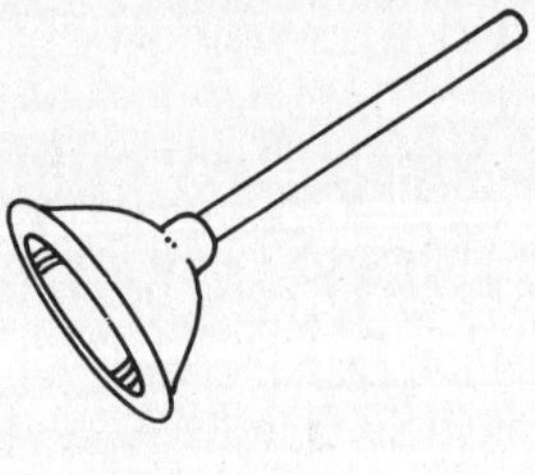

_____   _____   _____

_____   _____   _____

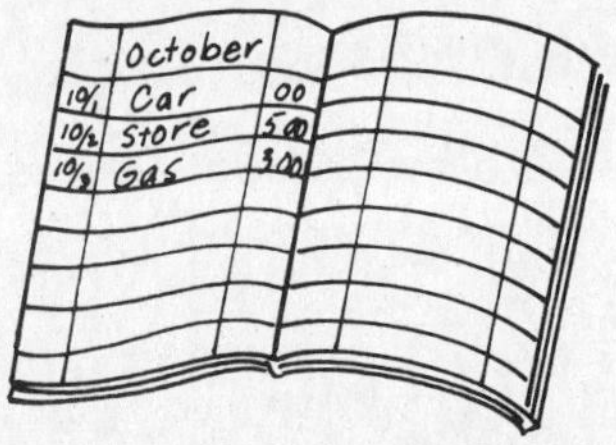

Soft g -ge- -gi-

Read the words in each box. Circle the word that names the picture.

margin
magnet
magic
Marge

dangle
damper
dancer
danger

ranger
stranger
danger
straggler

badger
badge
basket
batter

butter
budget
barge
bundle

racket
rancid
ranger
danger

Box in ge or gi in the words below. Read the words as you box in the letters.

stranger   tragic   danger   fidget   badger   Roger

budget   legend   plunger   margin   magic   urgent

Use the words above to fill in the blanks.

1. You may use this to fix stopped-up drains or pipes. _____

2. A very, very old story that may be partly true is called a _____.

3. This is a boy's or a man's name. _____

4. Something that must be done now and quickly is _____.

5. Pulling a rabbit out of an empty hat is a common _____ trick.

6. A plan showing how much you'll spend on different things. _____

7. The blank border around the writing on a page is the _____.

8. An animal with thick fur and short legs that burrows in the ground

   is a _____.

9. When there's a chance that you may be hurt or injured,

   you're in _____.

10. Something very, very sad may be called _____.

Soft g -ge- -gi-

Fill in **ge** in the words below. Write the correct word on the line under the pictures.

bud ___ ___ t   dan ___ ___ r   gad ___ ___ t   Ro ___ ___ r

_____   _____   _____

Fill in **gi** and write the correct word under the pictures.

mar ___ ___ n   fri ___ ___ d   tra ___ ___ c   ma ___ ___ c

_____   _____   _____ zone

Read the sentences. Write the correct word in each blank.

        changes   charges   channels

Marge often _____ the _____ on the TV set.

        ranch   rocket   ranger

The forest _____ told us about the fire by the _____.

        frigid   furnace   frozen

Last week our _____ broke down, and our house became

as _____ as the cold air outside.

        long   lender   legend

A _____ is a story first told in the past, _____, long ago.

        traffic   trace   tragic

It is _____ if someone is badly injured in _____.

Soft g variant endings

In these words the ending **age** sounds a little different from the word age, meaning how old someone is. Read these words and say them the way we do when we speak.

Look at the pictures. Read the sentence that tells about each picture.

This is **age.**

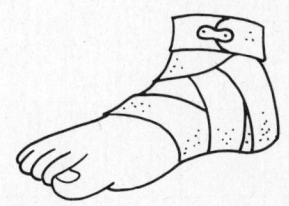

But this is **bandage.**

Box in   age   in these words. Read the words as you box in the letters.

cabbage   village   garbage   cottage   voyage

storage   garage   postage   message   luggage

Choose the correct word from above for each picture. Write it neatly on the line.

_____   _____   _____

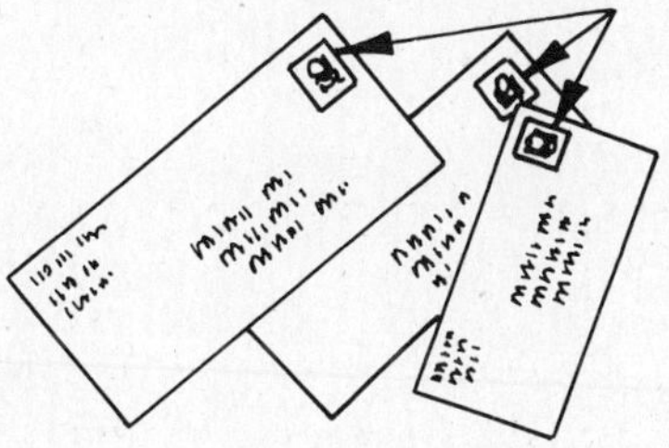

_____   _____   _____

_____   _____   _____

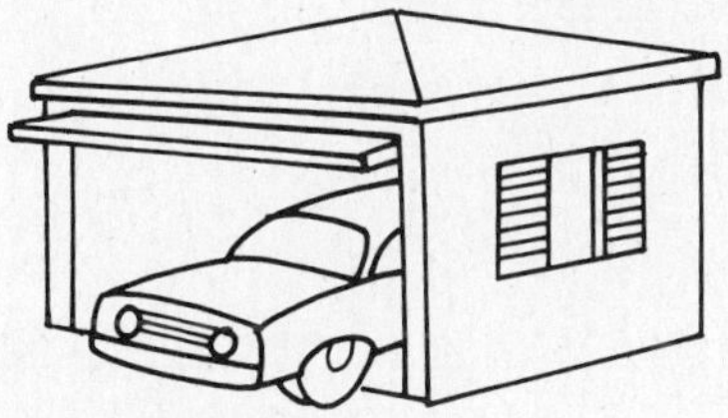

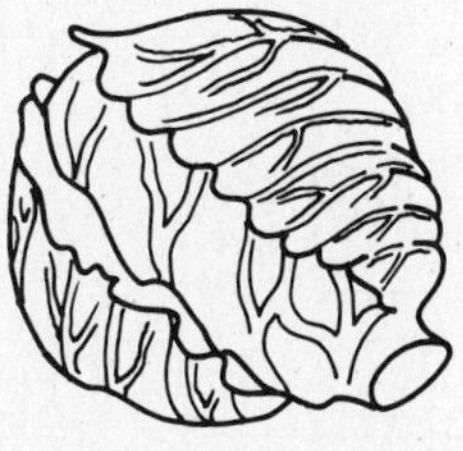

Soft g variant endings

Read the words in each box. Circle the word that names the picture.

cabbage college cottage cotton	frazzle freckle fringed fragile (fraj·l)	luggage lettuce lounge lunge
voyage vowel village voltage	collapse cottage collide college	empty enjoy engrave engine (en·jin)
passage package practice pocket	garbage garden gadget garage	message magic minute messy

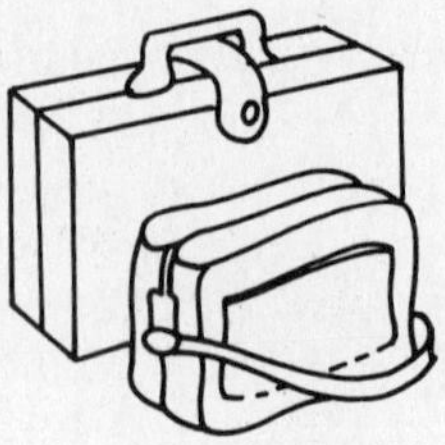

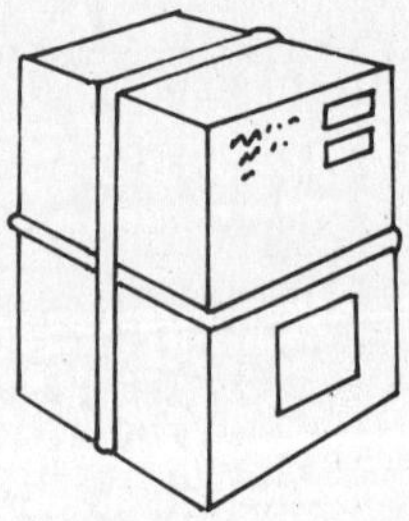

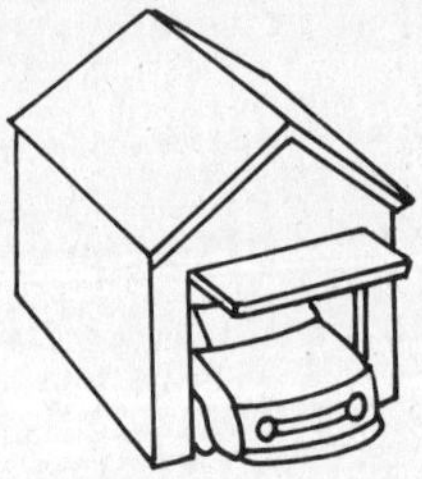

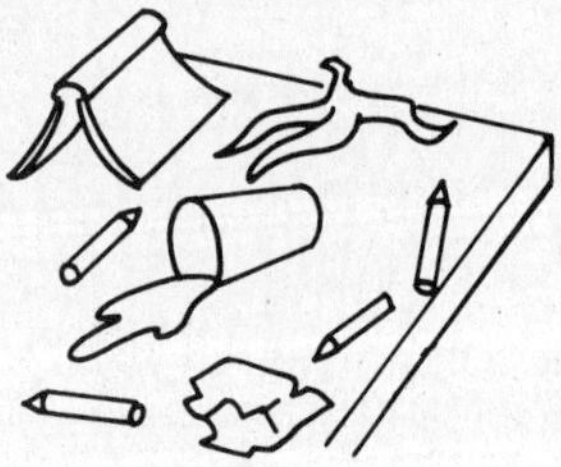

Box in ge or gi in the words below. Read the words as you box in the letters.

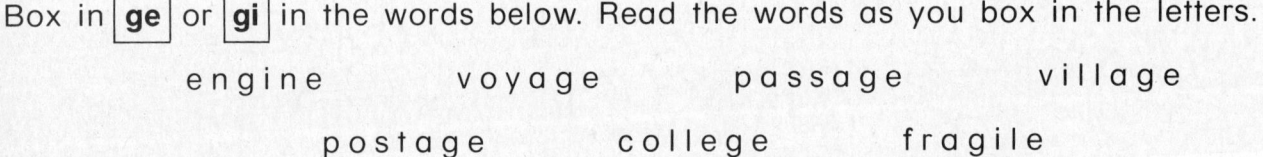

e n g i n e   v o y a g e   p a s s a g e   v i l l a g e

p o s t a g e   c o l l e g e   f r a g i l e

Use the words above to complete the sentences.

1. A school where adults may go is called a _____.

2. A long trip in a ship or spacecraft is called a _____.

3. A glass is _____, but a spoon is not.

4. A very small town is called a _____.

5. The part of the train that pulls all the cars is the _____.

6. A hallway or space for people to walk along may be called a _____

Soft g variant endings

Fill in **age** in the words below. Then write the correct word under each picture.

dam __ __ __ d   cabb __ __ __   bagg __ __ __   cott __ __ __

wreck __ __ __   post __ __ __   pack __ __ __   pass __ __ __

_____   _____   _____

_____   _____   _____

Read the sentences. Write the correct word in each blank.

garbage   gargle   garage

We keep our _____ cans next to the _____ .

water   wrinkled   wreckage

The _____ from the ship floated on the surface of the _____ .

visit   village   voyage

Long ago my grandfather went on a long sea _____ to _____
his uncle in Japan.

cottage   cackle   cotton

Jan made some _____ drapes for the windows in our _____ .

plastic   package   panther

The _____ of stickers was covered with clear, strong _____ .

messy   message   mistake

Mom left me a _____ to clean up my _____ room.

Soft g Hard g

Here are some words with soft g and some with g as in go. The g that sounds like the g in go is called **hard g**.

In the words below, box in hard g and the letter that follows it. Read all the words.

congress	engine	wage	glance	guppy	gurgle
grudge	gadget	arrange	giblets	stage	gem
garbage	tragic	gorge	goal	ranger	garlic

Find the words with soft g. Write them on the lines.

govern	_____	legend	_____	germs	_____
dodged		dragon		voyage	
glimpse	_____	seagull	_____	gamble	_____
ginger		pledge		pilgrim	
logic	_____	fragile	_____	college	_____
cigar		griddle		ignore	

Find the syllables that will complete these words. Write them on the lines.

gir _____	gent _____	ur _____
pas _____	en _____	stor _____
gin _____	rum _____	ger _____
ban _____	chal _____	gen _____
-sage, -affe, -dage, -ger	-gine, -mage, -ly, -lenge	-bil, -age, -tle, -gent

Add **-ger** or **-ged**

The beaver plun_____ into the river.

We used a plun_____ to clear the drain.

He is the best dod_____ on our team.

He dod_____ that fast ball very well.

Gene is the mana_____ of this store.

Last year he mana_____ another store.

Add **-ges** or **-ged**

Ginny has gone to buy two spon_____.

We all spon_____ up the paint mess.

The banda_____ are in the first-aid kit.

Roger banda_____ the cut on my wrist.

Sue dama_____ the bumper on her car.

They'll pay for all the dama_____.

Soft c and Soft g   **cy**   **gy**

The **gy** pattern is like ge and gi. It tells you to use soft g.
When you see **gy** at the end of a word, you—
1. Say the soft sound of g.
2. Say the vowel sound of y at the end of a two-syllable word.

Box in gy in the words below. Use the words to complete the sentences.

   d i n g y   s t i n g y   p u d g y

People who have plenty of cash but who hate to spend much are _____.

When white clothes begin to look gray, we say they are _____.

Sometimes we say that a chubby puppy is cute and _____ .

In the words below, you see **cy** and **gy** at the beginning of the word. The **cy** or **gy** at the beginning of a word tells you to—
1. Say the soft sound of c or g.
2. Read the y with the same vowel sound as i in sit.

Box in gy or cy in these words. Write the words under the correct pictures.

   g y m n a s t   g y p s y   c y m b a l s   g y m

_____   _____   _____   _____

Use the words above to fill in the blanks.

Every Thursday afternoon Bruce's _____ class plays basketball.

A _____ is very skilled at tumbling and doing handstands on the bars.

Cindy plays the _____ in our school's marching band.

A member of a roaming tribe of people known for their songs and

dances. _____

Soft g   Hard g

In the words below, you see **ge** or **gi** followed by an o. When you see **geo** or **gio**, you keep ge or gi together to make soft g. Then o is the vowel you use in reading the word.

Box in ge or gi in the words below. Use the words to fill in the blanks.

dungeon   pigeons   regions

surgeon   George   sturgeon

1. You see many of these large birds in the city; they are _____.

2. A doctor who can take out someone's tonsils is a _____.

3. A very large fish that fishermen enjoy catching is a _____.

4. A strong underground room used long ago for prisoners is a _____.

5. A name that is often given to boys is _____.

6. Large parts of the world's surface, like deserts, are often called _____.

Here are words with **gu** followed by e, i, or y. In these words the u is silent, but it keeps the g away from the vowels so that you will use hard g. Then e, i, or y are the vowels you use in reading the word.

Box in the hard g pattern in the words below. Use the words to fill in the blanks.

guess   guilty   guitar   guinea

disguise   guest   guide   Guy

1. Here's the school where George takes _____ lessons.

2. I'm going to ask a good _____ to come with us when we explore those caves.

3. After the jury agreed that the man was not _____, the judge said he was free.

4. I'm going to keep Squeaky, who's the tamest of these four _____ pigs.

5. Let's try to _____ what's inside that package with the shiny wrapper.

6. A boy's or man's name that you don't hear very often is _____.

7. Our _____ is due to arrive at the airport on Tuesday at four o'clock.

8. The undercover police officer dressed in a workman's clothes

   as a _____.

Soft c   Soft g

These words have s in front of **ce** and **ci**. When the letters **sce** or **sci** stand together, they make the soft c pattern.

Box in sce or scj in the words below. Write the words under the correct pictures.

scene   scent   scissors   crescent

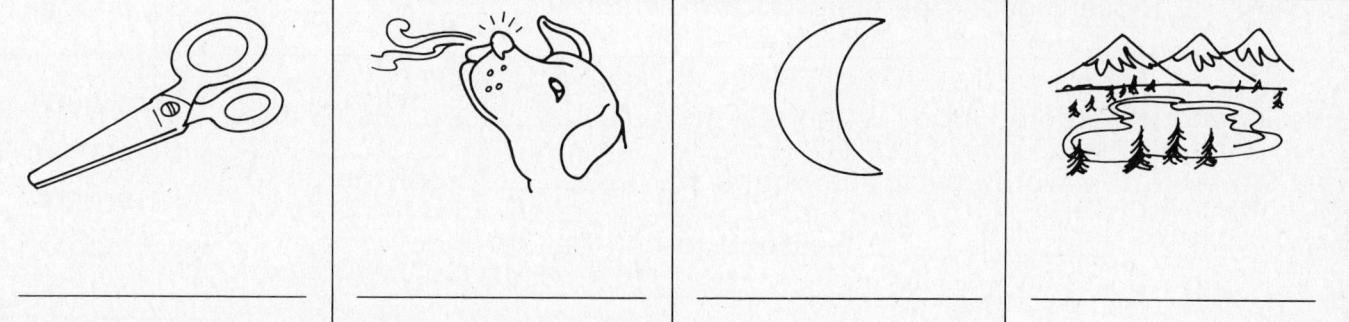

_____   _____   _____   _____

Use the words above to fill in the blanks.

1. A tool with two handles and two blades used for cutting is a _____.

2. Another word for a nice smell or a smell that is weak or faint is _____.

3. A part of an act in a play is called a _____.

4. When the moon is shaped like this ⟩, it is called a _____ moon.

These words have two **c**'s or two **g**'s in the middle. Divide them between the two middle consonants like this: ac|cent sug|gest. Circle the word that makes the sentence true.

The first syllable in accent has a (hard, soft) c.

The second syllable in accent has a (hard, soft) c.

The first syllable in suggest has a (hard, soft) g.

The second syllable in suggest has a (hard, soft) g.

Divide these words as you read them. Use them to complete the sentences.

accent   suggest   success   vaccine (vac·seen)   accept   succeed

1. I'm invited to George's birthday party and I'm going to _____.

2. My uncle was born and raised in Spain. He has a Spanish _____.

3. Doctors give people this so they won't get sick; it is a _____.

4. If you try very hard to do your best, you will _____.

5. I like to make masks, so I will _____ making them in art class.

6. Many people came and enjoyed the concert; it was a huge _____.

Soft g

Find the word that completes the sentence. Write it on the line.

Mrs. Poe's family enjoyed making peanut butter _____ yesterday.

Dad suggested I drive slowly on the icy surface of this _____.

Look at all those pigeons perched on that window _____!

| ledge |
| fudge |
| lounge |
| bridge |

The legend of "Robin Hood" is the tale he _____ us to read.

We will write the words by the left-hand _____ of the page.

Marcy left an _____ message to call her at once.

| urged |
| margin |
| urgent |
| magic |

A tow truck came after the crash and towed the _____ away.

I like the scent of the clean, fresh wood shavings in my guinea

pig's _____.

Henry hopes that the frost won't destroy or _____ our garden.

| cage |
| wreckage |
| stage |
| damage |

If you share cups with sick people, you may catch their _____.

The _____ did four cartwheels on the balance beam.

The nurse put the ointment on my scraped knee very _____.

| gentle |
| gymnast |
| gently |
| germs |

My skirt was wrinkled, so I _____ before going shopping.

The saleswoman made a mistake and _____ the wrong price.

Putting that model spaceship together will be a _____.

| challenge |
| arrange |
| changed |
| charged |

Lately I've had car problems, so I want the _____ tuned up.

Bleach makes clothes look whiter when they become _____.

The plastic dishes Mom buys aren't _____ like glass.

| fragile |
| stingy |
| engine |
| dingy |

Howard washed the shower tiles, wiped them dry, and wrung out

the _____.

Mrs. Knox will _____ a surprise party for her husband.

The lakes and hills in this _____ of our state make it pretty.

| arrange |
| ranger |
| sponge |
| region |

Soft c   Soft g
Adding **-ing** or **-y** to base words that end with –ce or –ge

When you add **-ing** or **-y** to vowel-consonant-vowel words that end in e, like lace, leave out the e and add **-ing** to get lacing or add **-y** to get lacy. This keeps the vowel-consonant-vowel pattern. When you see the vowel-consonant-vowel pattern, you say the vowel name (the long vowel sound).

Box in the vowel-consonant-vowel pattern in the words below. Find the base word and write it on the line. The example (ex·am·ple) shows you what to do.

raging	icing	facing	aging	slicing	tracing
rage	_____	_____	_____	_____	_____

icy	paging	lacing	lacy	racing	placing
_____	_____	_____	_____	_____	_____

Circle the correct word and write it on the line.

1. I suggest you use this pencil for _____ those pictures.
   (traceing, tracing)

2. Our school's eighth grade is _____ a play.
   (staging, stageing)

3. Their two teams were _____ across the gym.
   (racing, raceing)

4. Dad is _____ the roast for our dinner guests.
   (sliceing, slicing)

5. Some people think _____ wild animals is wrong.
   (cageing, caging)

6. They are _____ the clothes they'll be selling at their garage sale.
   (priceing, pricing)

Use the words below to complete the sentences.

   placing   raging   spacing   facing   icing   paging

1. George likes to have the desk in his room _____ the window.

2. Grace is _____ a knife, a fork, and a spoon by each person's plate.

3. She likes to eat the _____ off the top of her cake first.

4. Evan said, "I hear them _____ Dr. Spencer on the loudspeaker."

5. Janice has problems correctly _____ her words when she writes.

Words that do not follow the soft g rule

Many words do not follow the rule that tells you to use soft g when you see **ge**, **gi**, and **gy**. You know many of these words. Read the words below and sort them into lists that show which words follow the ge, gi, and gy rule and which words do not.

List the words that follow the **ge**, **gi**, and **gy** rule.

		Soft g as in gentle, giraffe
begin	lounge	
gem	gift	_____ _____
longer	bandage	_____ _____
stingy	finger	_____ _____
urgent	geese	_____ _____
eager	strange	_____ _____
give	gym	
package	larger	

List the words that <u>do not</u> follow the **ge**, **gi**, and **gy** rule.

		Hard g as in go
anger	ginger	
fragile	foggy	_____ _____
girl	wage	_____ _____
target	engine	_____ _____
ledge	druggist	_____ _____
forgive	gadget	_____ _____
dungeon	biggest	
giggle	shaggy	

Add **-ger** or **-ges**	Add **-ged** or **-ges**
We write our expenses in a led_____.	Bruce is one of the dog show jud_____.
The bad_____ is a burrowing animal.	They char_____ a lot for the meal.
The scouts got their bad_____ today.	I jud_____ the pies at the State Fair.
Outside of windows are led _____.	The store now char_____ for gift boxes.
Grass along sidewalks is trimmed with	The leaves on some plants have sharp
an ed_____.	ed_____.

Sight Words 3: eyes, been, shoes, door, floor

Read the sentences. The meaning of the sentence will help you read the word in the box. Below each set of sentences, circle all the words that match the sample word.

One | eye | is closed.

Close one eye. Can you still see? _____

These are her | eyes |.

What color are your eyes? _____

| eyes | yes | eyes | yams | eyes | eggs | eaves | eyes | ears |

Will she be the winner?

Have you ever | been | in a race? _____

He has | been | sick for a week.

Have you been sick often? _____

| been | bean | beam | been | deer | been | need | been | bees |

She has one | shoe | on.

Do shoe stores sell ice cream? _____

Now she has both | shoes | on.

Do your gym shoes have laces? _____

| shoes | shows | shoes | shore | shove | shoes | hoes | shoes | does |

She closes the | door |.

Do some cars have four doors? _____

He sweeps the | floor |.

Do you walk on a floor? _____

| door | door | deer | droop | doom | boar | door | done | door |
| floor | flour | fool | four | floor | flow | floor | foot | floor |

Sight Words 3: eyes, been, shoes, door, floor

Write the correct word on the line under each picture.

eye	shoes	foot	eyes
door	floor	shoe	road

_____   _____   _____   _____

Use these words to fill in the blanks below.

been	slippers	teeth	bent	legs	shoes	shells	eye
floor	houses	door	chair	four	eyes	desk	shoe

1. Gerbils, squirrels, and mice all have tails and four _____.

2. This is often made of wood; it has hinges and a knob. _____

3. I've _____ looking everywhere for those large scissors!

4. Lobsters, oysters, and turtles all have _____.

5. This is often made of wood and is used to sit on. _____

6. Carmen wanted all of the pipe cleaners that weren't _____.

7. All animals, including giraffes, guinea pigs, and birds, have two _____.

8. People may put these on their feet when they go outside. _____

9. This is made of wood and is often covered with a carpet. _____

10. Some people put these on their feet when they lounge at home. _____

11. Once a year Grandmother goes to Dr. George for an _____ exam.

12. I wanted to buy a pair of boots, so I went to a _____ store.

13. Animals live outdoors, but people live in _____.

14. Mr. and Mrs. Knox have two girls and two boys; they have _____ children.

15. If you want to eat an apple, you take a bite with your _____.

Sight Words 3: eyes, been, shoes, door, floor

Circle the word that belongs in the sentence.

Don't forget to close the (floor, door, roof) behind you when you leave.

They enjoy playing with their trucks on the kitchen (door, room, floor).

Your (eyes, ears, nose) are that part of your body that you see with.

Has the gerbil (bean, been, need) put back into its cage?

My sister suggested I buy this purse to go with my black (socks, shows, shoes).

Has that little squirrel (seen, been, gone) injured?

Tie the laces of your (shoes, hood, eyes) to keep your ears covered.

Gene has gone to get the sponge mop to clean up the (door, four, floor).

When you wink, you close one (door, mouth, eye).

The entrance to an office or home is the (door, window, floor).

We've (done, been, seen) at the cottage this week, painting the dingy kitchen walls.

Vince got out of the car to raise the garage (door, floor, roof).

When you bounce a ball, you use your hand and (foot, eyes, ears).

Tie the laces of your gym (shirt, shoes, jacket) so you won't trip.

Alice let both of her pet guinea pigs run around on her bedroom (door, wall, floor).

Do you know who hasn't (done, seen, been) to the magic show yet?

People's (eyes, shoes, dresses) are never orange or purple.

It's best to put on (shoes, boots, slippers) to play in deep snow.

That must be our guests ringing the (floor, door, room) bell.

Please don't leave your clothes lying on your bedroom (roof, flour, floor).

Mr. Rice said we can't be in the races unless our (racket, ball, shoes) are tied.

I guess this pair of sandals belongs in that blue (cigar, shoe, match) box.

Adding endings to base words that end with <u>consonant –y</u>

Most words that end with **-ies,** like <u>tries</u>, <u>flies</u>, and <u>spies</u>, come from a base word that ends with a <u>consonant</u> and <u>y</u>.

Box in the <u>consonant –y</u> pattern in these words: d⌐r y⌐   f l y   s k y   s p y

Read these sentences. Look at how the words with the boxed-in letters have changed. Circle the correct answer.

People f|ly| in planes.   Do you think a jet plane **flies** fast?   yes   no

Children will c|ry| .   Do you think an infant **cries** when hungry?   yes   no

> **RULE:** To add **-s** to words that end with a <u>consonant</u> and <u>y</u>, change <u>y</u> to <u>i</u> and add **-es.**

Follow the RULE above and add **-s** to the words below. Write the words you make on the lines.

dry _____   fly _____   fry _____   pry _____

cry _____   spy _____   sky _____   try _____

Use <u>any</u> of the words above to complete these sentences. Answer the questions.

If she shares her French _____ , is she stingy?   yes   no

Will he need a tool to _____ the lid off a can?   yes   no

If a dog _____ to fly, will it succeed?   yes   no

To find the base word, <u>cross out</u> **-es** and change <u>i</u> back to <u>y</u>. Do this to these words.

ski̶e̶s̶   sky _____   pries _____   dries _____   fries _____

cries _____   spies _____   tries _____   flies _____

Use <u>any</u> of the words above to complete these sentences. Answer the questions.

Will a little boy _____ when he is hurt?   yes   no

Can _____ bother a family picnic?   yes   no

Will a kitchen floor still be wet after it is _____?   yes   no

---

Find the words that end with a <u>consonant</u> and <u>y</u>. Box in the <u>consonant –y</u>. Add **s** to <u>just those</u> words. Write the words you make on the lines. Follow the RULE above.

s p y _____   s t r a y _____   c r y _____   e n j o y _____

b u y _____   d r y _____   f l y _____   e m p l o y _____

Adding endings to base words that end with consonant -y

Words that end with **-ied,** like fried and spied, come from a base word that ends with a consonant and y.

Read these sentences. Look at how the words with the boxed-in letters have changed. Circle the correct answer.

He'll f|ry| the chicken.   Do people like to eat **fried** chicken?   yes   no

Grapes are left in the sun to d|ry| .   Are raisins **dried** grapes?   yes   no

RULE: When you add **-ed** to words that end with a consonant and y, change y to i and add **-ed**.

Follow the RULE above and add **-ed** to the words below. Write the words you make on the lines.

cry   cried   dry _____   pry _____

fry _____   spy _____   try _____

Use any of the words above to complete these sentences. Answer the questions.

When you _____ on the shoes, did you put them on your feet?   yes   no

If he _____ on someone, did he watch him closely?   yes   no

If you _____ the lid off a can, will it still be closed?   yes   no

To find the base word, cross out **-ed** and change i back to y. Do this to these words.

dried _____   cried _____   spied _____

pried _____   tried _____   fried _____

Use any of the words above to complete these sentences. Answer the questions.

Will wet clothes _____ on a clothesline?   yes   no

Was Nancy happy if she _____ ?   yes   no

When you _____ the fish yesterday, did you cook it?   yes   no

Find the words that end with a consonant and y. Box in the consonant -y pattern. Add **ed** to just those words and write them on the lines. Follow the RULE above.

c r y   _____   s t a y _____   p r y _____   d i s p l a y _____

a n n o y _____   t r y _____   f r y _____   d e s t r o y _____

Adding endings to base words that end with <u>consonant</u> –y

Look at the last two letters of the words below. How many words end with a <u>consonant</u> and y? _____ How many words end with a <u>vowel</u> and y? _____

study   daisy   annoy   lily   candy   fairy   stay

_____

Remember the RULE about adding **-s** or **-ed** when you do this part.

Add **-s**	Add **-ed**	Write the Base Word
penny _pennies_	study _____	stories _____
worry _____	dirty _____	muddied _____
city _____	play _____	flurries _____
buy _____	pity _____	destroys _____
guppy _____	empty _____	worried _____

_____

When you add **-ing** to words that end with y, you <u>do not change any letters</u> in the base word. Add **-ing** to the words below.

study_____   hurry_____   copy_____   spy_____

enjoy_____   empty_____   worry_____   dry_____

_____

Use the words below to fill in the blanks in the sentences.
Write the base word in the blank at the end of each sentence.

worries   hurried   tried   daisies
fireflies   fried   dairies   lilies

1. I changed my mind and ordered oatmeal with milk rather than

   _____ eggs.   _____

2. I'm going to arrange that bunch of _____ in this vase.   _____

3. If I don't call when I'm going to be late, my mom _____.   _____

4. We were late, so we knocked on the door and _____ in.   _____

5. Milk products like butter and cheese are made in _____.   _____

6. After dark in the summertime, we see many _____.   _____

7. I _____ hard and I got the knots out of my shoelaces.   _____

8. There were dragonflies at the pond by the water _____.   _____

Adding endings to base words that end with <u>consonant -y</u>

Read each sentence. Choose the best word for the sentence. Write it on the line.

We're _____ to get to the ice-cream truck before it pulls away. He wants to be finished painting by Saturday, so he'll _____. I called for some help, and Mom _____ to see what was wrong.	hurry hurries hurried hurrying
Mr. Turner is going to pass out _____ of the story you wrote. My little sister keeps _____ everything that I do. I know you like the picture I took, so I'll get a _____ for you.	copy copies copied copying
Richard sharpened his pencil before he began _____ again. Robin's brother kept annoying her while she tried to _____. Steven goes into his bedroom and closes the door when he _____.	study studies studied studying
We won't use the front porch until the paint _____. The front grass _____ faster than the back because it's in the sun. Dad suggested placing the wet firewood in the garage to _____.	dry dries dried drying
Justin was _____ his knapsack to make room for his gym shoes. On Thursdays, my brother _____ the wastebaskets in the house. Mom _____ her purse when she was trying to find a pencil.	empty empties emptied emptying
A jet plane _____ long distances in a short length of time. In the fall, flocks of wild geese _____ south for the winter. Who's that player who is so good at catching _____ balls?	fly fly flies flying
Use a sponge to wipe the floor that Ed's muddy shoes _____. Don't let the children put their _____ hands on the windows. Dad was annoyed at Burt for _____ his clean white shirt.	dirty dirties dirtied dirtying

© 1995 SRA/McGraw-Hill

Review 3

Circle the correct word.

Boys, girls, men, women are .... children   birds   people   animals

To wiggle around is to .... squirm   destroy   injure   race

A cage is a place to keep .... daisies   coins   animals   cigars

---

To purchase means to .... join   suggest   buy   appoint

A bird that can't fly is the .... pigeon   ostrich   eagle   crow

This is a girl's name. .... Edward   George   Robert   Joyce

---

Something strange is .... strong   odd   common   fancy

To pursue means to .... race   guess   chase   disturb

These can make you sick. .... germs   gems   doctor   nurse

---

A car is kept in a .... house   attic   dungeon   garage

This is a tool. .... toy   wrench   knot   metal

These may be played in a band. .... stories   shiny   cymbals   shoes

---

A very small town is a .... city   state   mayor   village

This is a boy's name. .... Helen   Marge   Roger   Colleen

A parcel is a .... clothes   shoe   package   guitar

---

Another word for voyage is .... luggage   door   trip   gone

A waltz is a kind of .... game   dance   food   party

Hail is rain frozen into balls of .... rubber   golf   ice   melt

---

Clifford goes camping with a .... knob   wrench   knapsack   wrapper

Eyes can't be .... closed   blue   square   large

Doors and floors can be made of .... concrete   wood   foil   cement

People polish shoes when they're .... shiny   magic   soil   dirty

Review 3

Read the question. Underline the words that answer the question.

Which of these animals are covered with fur?

hamster	turtle	beaver	ostrich	muskrat	oyster
lizard	panther	robin	pigeon	lobster	guinea pig
weasel	giraffe	snail	squirrel	gerbil	crow

Which of these may be found inside a school?

gym	crayons	thermos	garage	pencils	playground
folders	stroller	ruler	concert	igloo	mattress
children	books	dungeon	scissors	studies	workbooks

Which of these animals can be kept as pets?

beaver	goldfish	hamster	panther	ostrich	kitten
guppies	oyster	muskrat	puppies	gerbil	owl
giraffe	lobster	mouse	crab	squirrel	camel

Which of these are living things?

birds	guitars	women	ice	reptiles	dirt
shoes	shrubs	floors	bushes	pennies	daisies
people	worms	boys	furnaces	animals	purse

Which of these are foods?

broil	custard	ketchup	foil	cabbage	french fries
pumpkin	rice	ice cream	burnt	churn	oven
lettuce	slurp	poison	turnip	raisins	spicy

Which animals live in water and have shells?

trout	clam	perch	snake	crab	baboon
turtle	guppies	beaver	oyster	lobster	muskrat
frog	shark	shrimp	camel	whale	goldfish

140

Review 3

Circle the words in the box below that have something to do with being <u>sick or well</u>.
Use them to complete these sentences.

We're convinced that Dr. Rogers, whose office is upstairs, is a fine _____.

The nurse said that people are given shots of _____ so they won't get ill.

Let's wash our hands before we cook to get all the dirt and _____ off.

vaccine	danger	guests	germs	surgeon	stranger	guide	voyage

Now underline the words above that tell about <u>people</u>. Use them to fill in the blanks.

Someone who's not known to us is called a _____.

If you invite people to your home, they're your _____.

Someone who knows the way and leads others so they don't get lost. _____

Circle the words in the box below that have to do with the <u>mail</u>.
Use them to fill in the blanks.

The cost of postal service that we pay for by buying stamps. _____

A wrapped package that can be sent by mail is called a _____.

A way to let someone know something is to write a note with your _____.

parcel	charge	dingy	postage	stingy	budget	poster	message

Now underline the words above that have something to do with how people <u>spend their cash</u>. Use them to complete the sentences below.

If someone hates to spend any cash, we often say that person is _____.

Dad plans what he's going to do with his wages in our family's _____.

The clerk said if I want my package gift-wrapped, there will be a small

_____.

Write the base word for the words below. Read the words.

poppies _____ fried _____ emptied _____

candied _____ cries _____ hobbies _____

buggies _____ jellied _____ dries